The Twelve Apostles of Jesus

Their Forgotten History

#

Dr. Richard Orzeck

Purrfect Love Publishing
2088 Trumansburg Road
Trumansburg, NY 14886
USA

ISBN-13: 9781541181571
First Edition

Dedication

To my mother
Mary Orzeck
1932 – 2017

Thank you for giving us life!

Table of Contents:

Introduction

Several years ago, my wife and I made a trip to Rome, Italy. Our goal was to see as many of the tourist attractions in that glorious and eternal city as possible. After navigating the many tourist land mines associated with a visit to the Coliseum (pickpockets, panhandlers, and extortionist Roman gladiator models), of eating the world's best gelato and sipping overpriced coffee at the Trevi fountain, and of visiting the *Ossa et Cineres* (bones and ashes) of the painter Raphael at the Pantheon, we made a pilgrimage to the Vatican and St. Peter's Basilica. After attending the English Mass at St. Peter's, we made our way into the catacombs located below the main floor of the church. There we walked past the final resting places of many of Christianity's famous saints and the burial sites of several long-ago and long-deceased popes, including — at the time — that of the recently departed John Paul II. After some time, we eventually ended up in front of the gated tomb of Christianity's most famous saint, the apostle Peter.

What a thrill!

For an unknown number of minutes, we both lingered in front of the grave in silent awe. There we were . . . standing in front of the original "rock" as in, "Upon this rock I will build My Church." This was St. Peter: a man who was both severely rebuked and was infinitely loved by Jesus; a man who abandoned and denied our Lord at the time of His greatest need, but who later would become a loving and tireless

crusader on His behalf, and who would ultimately die a
martyr's death for the sake of his beloved friend. I knelt down at
the rail and strained my eyes to see if I could visualize anything
beyond the iron bars of the gate. I convinced myself that I could
see a small stone ossuary (box) sitting on a stone shelf. Although
I did say a couple of Our Fathers, I wasn't really praying; it was
more just me opening myself up to the sacredness of it all.

After several minutes, my wife Theresa gently mentioned
that we should move on. I found myself surprisingly reluctant
to do so. As would be the case with nearly all of my future visits
to the graves of the other Twelve Apostles, I was feeling an
overwhelming sense of gratitude and "oneness" with Peter.
That is, I was engulfed in the genuine spiritual presence of that
great man of God, and I didn't want to give it up!

But other pilgrims were also waiting to pay their
respects, and I eventually had to stand back up and step aside.
Before doing so, I literally thanked the apostle for everything he
did to spread the good news of Jesus Christ and for his ultimate
sacrifice for us all. And as the reality of being where I was
filtered back into my consciousness, I was struck with yet
another thought: I began to wonder out loud to Theresa where
the rest of these guys ended up.

Thus began my journey to visit as many of the places
associated with the Twelve Apostles as is humanly possible. My
task to become one with these great men would take me (and
my wife) to Europe, the Middle East, Asia, the subcontinent of
India, and even to Africa. Hours would be spent hunting down
leads in translations of the ancient books, following up ancient
local and Church traditions, and poring over an endless number
of websites. To the best of my research and intuition, I have
visited and experienced spiritually — as of this writing — all but
two (Jude's and Matthew's) of the original martyrdom sites of
the Twelve. The same is true of their original burial sites. And I
have done pilgrimage to each and every one of their present-
day tombs and several of their minor shrines. Since the original
Pentecost of over two thousand years ago, I don't believe any

one person alive or dead — not even our beloved pope(s) — can make the claim that they were in the physical presence of all Twelve Apostles.

This quest has been a genuine labor of love. Studying the stories of these twelve men, learning of their personal and physical struggles, sharing in their humanity, and sensing their spiritual essences as I stood near their mortal remains, I feel as if they are now all my dear, dear friends . . . almost brothers! My sincerest hope for this book is to share this great blessing I've been given with you all.

A Defense and a Non-apology

Before beginning, I need to address the following issue. I'll add, also, that many of my predecessors over the last fifty years who wrote previous books on the lives of the Twelve Apostles of Jesus felt this same responsibility. Additionally, because most of these authors were members of the Reformed Christian tradition (Protestant, Baptist, Evangelical, etc.), they seemed to feel the obligation to do so even more. The issue I'm speaking of is: Why should anyone bother at all to document the lives of these dead men; why even care where or how they died; or, even more worthless in the big scheme of things, why be concerned about where their dusty old bones are today?

I've learned that there is a belief among some Christian sects that all that truly matters is the Living Word of God that the Twelve shared with the world during their ministries; that choosing to be in the physical presence of these great men — and all of the other Christian saints and martyrs as well — is a complete waste of time; that in some extreme interpretations, the veneration of these relics is somehow a form of pagan ancestor worship. Of course, many learned and well-intentioned Christians on both sides of the matter have many scriptural quotes and Church traditions to back them up. But I'm not going to go there; it's a theological minefield that I don't wish to waste time trying to cross. I will just say that if that's the sincere way a reader of this book feels, it's not my place to argue with you.

But I would ask: Whenever I stop on my drive down to New York City to visit my mother's grave in Florida, New York, or my dad's in the veterans' cemetery outside of Ocala, Florida, does that mean I'm worshiping them? Or if I visit the tomb of President Kennedy in Arlington? Or the Vietnam Veterans Memorial? Or the fallen sailors and marines at the battleship *Arizona*? Or, perhaps, even the grave of Jim Morrison in Paris? Of course not! I visit all of the above (and more) in order to honor their memories, reflect upon their lives, and in many cases, take in a bit of their spirit. If I happen to want to say a few prayers, not a soul on this earth has the right to stop me or to tell me I'm "worshiping" these people!

As I stated earlier, my primary intention for this quest was to gather whatever knowledge I could on these twelve men and to share it with the world. My main intention is for this to be a history book. Having done my best to do so, I freely admit that whenever I was in their presence either at their martyrdom sites, shrines, original tombs, or final graves, I did say a few prayers. Although I could have done so, I never asked for their intercession in any particular matter. (I have my own list of saints for that purpose.) Rather, I just said hello, took in emotionally and spiritually the honor and experience of being in their presence, and then I humbly thanked them for their great work in the service of the Lord.

An Acknowledgment

In the last fifty years most of the books published on the lives of the Twelve Apostles were written by theologians, by theological academics, and even a sitting pope. One of the more recent books was even written by a self-described atheist. It is with the valuable help of these books—and the World Wide Web—that I launched my original investigations. And it is for their pioneering scholarship that I am eternally thankful.

However, with the partial exception of the book, *In Search of the Twelve Apostles* by the late Dr. William McBirnie, the main problem I had with these books was that I learned almost nothing about the Twelve. After each of these books' authors stated a few basic historical facts of an apostle's life, they then progressed to citing lengthy tomes of theology. Infinitely more important, it appears that Dr. McBirnie and I were the only writers who obtained a large quantity of our knowledge by actually visiting and immersing ourselves in the places and local culture associated with the Twelve.

It is this gap in the knowledge of the actual lives, missions, martyrdoms, postmortem journeys, and final resting places of these great men — men who were chosen by the Lord Himself — that I try my best to address in this book. I want this to be a book of their biographies. I'm letting their hopes and fears and occasional misunderstandings of their Master's Word speak for the genuineness of their humanity. I let their love for the Risen Lord and their selfless dedication to the spreading of His Gospel be the shining light that illuminates their lives. I do, occasionally, quote a limited amount of "chapter and verse" but only to place each apostle into the context of the big picture.

In the spirit of full disclosure, I'd like to share just a few details about myself as they pertain to the creation of this book. As of this writing, I am a practicing veterinarian, world traveler, wildlife photographer, scuba diver, amateur folklorist, and avid reader of nonfiction. Both my wife and I are practicing Catholics who often go on pilgrimages to places important not only to our own faith but to many of the world's great religious and spiritual traditions as well. But what makes me uniquely qualified to attempt a book like this is my ability to be objective about the whole subject.

By this I mean that as much as I love my Christian faith — and all of the world's religious beliefs in general — I am still a trained man of science. My college degrees in biology and medicine have given me the skills to pursue endless hours of mundane research. More importantly, this training has given me the ability to observe with the critical eye of a healer the theological bias of both the ancient and the relatively recent writers, and to ferret out intentionally hidden details resulting from the tiresome political power grabs that underlay the claims of the various Christian denominations from over their last 2,000-plus-year history. My ultimate goal is to, hopefully, extract from this often conflicting information a detached and unbiased conclusion that is fair to all faiths and denominations and that recognizes the contributions of all members of my beloved Christian family.

I conclude this section of the book by sharing the following thoughts. The only thing anyone can say with 100 percent certainty with regards to the fate of any of the Twelve Apostles of Jesus is that James, the son of Zebedee and brother of John, was beheaded by Herod in Jerusalem. Period. All else that has been said about these men is from second- and third- and fourth-hand sources that can all be subject to various interpretations.

From the very beginning of the writing of this book, my intention was to make it readable to a general audience. Biblical scholars who may take the time to read it may note my lack of citations and footnotes. I've intentionally not included these hallmarks of academic necessity for a couple of reasons: First and foremost, is that the vast majority of books that include such things tend to be boring as heck to everyone except other scholars and theologians. And when they are included, these same scholars and theologians will then use these citations and footnotes to intellectually "beat the author over the head" in order to discredit his or her work.

The second reason is that in order to provide a clean and smooth, birth-to-death life's journey for each of these twelve men, some details required original research and consideration. For example, history is silent as to how the bones of the apostle Simon made it from the modern-day nation of Abkhazia into the hands of King Charlemagne in order for the king to be able to donate these relics to both the Vatican and the Basilica of St.

Sernin in Toulouse. By extensively studying the historical record, I believe I discovered how.

Another example is: Where exactly on the island of Chios, Greece, did the apostle Thomas's mortal remains rest for over one hundred years before being stolen and brought to Italy? Nearly every single theological scholar states that his relics spent some time on the island, but not a single one states where. I went to Chios and am now able to fill in this missing link.

Although there are many more examples, a final one involved the precise location of the apostle Bartholomew's martyrdom. In the literature, there were two competing places: the town of Baskale in southeastern Turkey and Baku, the modern-day capital of Azerbaijan. With great difficulty, after visiting both places, I came to the fairly easy conclusion that it was Baskale. I say this because there is the ruin of a huge Armenian basilica on the site that local people there say has an unbroken history of being venerated as the place of martyrdom since the actual death of the apostle. Also (and I acknowledge that this is going to send some readers into a tizzy) when you are standing there in front of what used to be the main altar built over the place of Bartholomew's martyrdom, you can still actually feel the presence of that great man of God!

Who Were the Twelve Apostles of Jesus?

Before going much further in this book, when I speak of the Twelve Apostles of Jesus, I am referring only to the twelve men who were with Him during His entire earthly ministry *and* who were empowered with the gift of the Holy Spirit at the first Pentecost. Therefore, I'm excluding Judas Iscariot, the unfortunate apostle who had the tragic — but necessary — job of betraying the Lord, and I'm including Matthias, the apostle elected to be Judas's replacement. I'm also excluding St. Paul, whose life meets neither of the criteria.

The Twelve Apostles of Jesus were twelve unremarkable

Jewish men who literally walked upon the earth with the Son of God. They were fishermen, farmers, and a tax collector. None were scholars or politicians. They were all (except Matthias and Philip) personally chosen by Jesus Himself. They all listened to Him firsthand as he preached the Good News of the kingdom of God, and they were with Him as He worked His many miracles. They shared with Jesus their meals, their lodgings, and the sweat and dirt and all of the other hardships of being on the road. They were witnesses to His humanity with all of His human frustrations, His infinite love and understanding, and His occasional anger and personal grief. From the most mundane of tasks to the glory of His Resurrection, they were with Him. Their love for their friend Jesus and their good works on His behalf after His ascension into heaven would cause them all great personal suffering and, ultimately, their dedication would cost them all their lives.

However, as ordinary as these twelve men were, they would change the course of world history. And surprisingly, we know almost nothing definitive about most of them! With the exception of a few cameo appearances in the Gospels, the beheading of James the Greater, and a few allusions of Peter being in Rome, the New Testament is silent on the Twelve. Most of what we know of these men is from the conflicted writings of the early Church fathers and historians, several apocryphal documents, and a rich collection of local traditions.

The reasons for this historical oversight are a matter of great speculation. Early Christianity's history prior to the various Ecumenical councils and its struggles with its numerous Orthodox and Gnostic sects likely started the problem. Political intrigues and the various power struggles between the Church of Rome and the Church of Constantinople that lead to the Great East vs. West Schism of 1054 made the situation worse. Then throw into the mix the various invasions by the barbarians, the Huns, the Muslims, and the Crusaders, along with the resulting destruction of libraries and universities and churches, and it is easy to understand how a lot of the knowledge of the apostles could be lost.

There's also a simpler reason for their being overlooked. This is that the apostles' main purpose was to concentrate on teaching the known world of both the humanity of Jesus Christ as well as His divine mission as the savior of mankind. The apostles (and all of the other disciples of Jesus) were to be merely His messengers for spreading the Gospel and to pass along their apostolic authority to future Christian leaders. Nothing sinister; maybe it just happened that no one thought to take the time to write down their stories.

A Note on the Photographs

Unless otherwise stated, all photos were taken by the author and his wife, Theresa. Pictures of all of several of the paintings were downloaded from Wikicommons. There are approximately twelve photos I had had to purchase from the stock photography company, Shutterstock. And there were three pictures given to me by a dear friend and fellow traveler, Laurant Derame.

The Apostle Peter Holding the Keys to the Kingdom
Shutterstock

Chapter One
The Apostle Peter 31 YRS

"But what about you?" He asked. "Who do you say I am?" Simon Peter answered, "You are the Messiah, the Son of the living God." Jesus replied, "Blessed are you, Simon son of Jonah, for this was not revealed to you by flesh and blood, but by my Father in heaven. And I tell you that you are Peter, and on this rock I will build my church ..." Matthew 16:15–18 NIV

The Gospel of John tells us that the apostle Simon Peter was the son of Jonah and the brother of the apostle Andrew. At the time they received their calling to be disciples of Jesus, both men were living in the small Galilean fishing village of Bethsaida. And it is with this most innocent of references in St. John's Gospel that the historical confusion regarding the life of Peter begins. This is because modern-day researchers cannot even agree on the exact location of which John is speaking when he said "Bethsaida." Therefore, until the archaeologists decide for sure, I'll just say that Peter was born in a fishing village on the north shore of the Sea of Galilee near where the Jordan River flows into it.

Peter makes many appearances in the four Gospels, mostly as one of the three apostles that Jesus seemed to treat as his inner circle (the other two inner-circle members being James and John, the sons of Zebedee). He traveled extensively with Jesus and the other apostles throughout the regions of Judea, Samaria, and Galilee. The farthest north they all traveled together that is mentioned in the New Testament is Caesarea-Philippi, located at the base of Mt. Herman in present-day Israel; in the south, they ventured as far as the Judea wilderness near the north and west shores of the Dead Sea.

Caesarea-Philippi: Temple of Pan
Shutterstock

After Pentecost, Peter took charge of the early Christian Church in Jerusalem until the time James the Just became her bishop. The book of Acts records several of Peter's local missionary journeys to the surrounding region. One of the first trips mentioned is to Samaria (the town of Samaria, not the region). Known today as the village of Sebastia, it was there that Peter and John encountered and defeated Simon the Sorcerer. Next, the book of Acts has Peter traveling to the town of Lydda (the modern-day city of Lod), where he cures a paralyzed man named Aeneas. Acts 9:36–41 tells of his travels to the town of Joppa (modern-day Jaffa) to raise the disciple Tabitha from the dead. It was in Joppa, as well, while he was staying at the home of Simon the tanner, that Peter had his vision in which a voice told him, "Do not call anything impure that God has made clean."

The apostle is then summoned by Cornelius the centurion — who, himself, had a dream at the same time as Peter did — to the soldier's home in the Mediterranean port city of Caesarea. It was there that this Roman officer was baptized by Peter and became the first uncontested Gentile to convert to the new faith of Christianity. Acts 12:17 states that while with the disciples at the house of Mary, the mother of John, Peter told the assembled anxious listeners, "Tell James and the other brothers and sisters about this [his having just escaped from prison in Jerusalem]," and then he left for another place.

"And then he left for another place." With that simple and highly imprecise statement, not another conclusive word is written in the New Testament regarding Peter's future missionary travels.

Although it is not precisely clear in the book of Acts, it is thought (with the exception of James the Less) that after the final Apostolic Council in Jerusalem in 50 AD that those of the

---

A Point to Ponder

• The Greco Roman city of Caesarea-Philippi (modern-day Banias) was the furthest north Jesus had traveled in the company of the Twelve Apostles. It was in that region of northern Israel twenty-five miles north of the Sea of Galilee that Matthew's Gospel says that Jesus revealed He would establish a Church and that He would give primacy over it to the apostle Peter. Much has been written over the millennia speculating as to why Jesus chose this place to make this important announcement. One interesting opinion I discovered in my researches for this book I found very intriguing.

• In ancient times, Caesarea-Philippi was a cultic center for the worship many of the Greek and Roman gods. There was even a temple complex built in honor of the Greek god Pan in a rocky grotto from which flowed the source of the Jordon River. It is this association with the pagan Gentiles that perhaps inspired Jesus to select this spot for this most important of pronouncements. On its surface, the meaning of "and on this rock I will build my Church" is quite clear. He was talking directly to the apostle Simon Peter (afterwards known only as Peter). But to add a deeper and more inclusive meaning to His statement, imagine that at the same time He was talking to Peter, He also turned toward the Gentile temples in the rocky cliffs behind them to indicate symbolically His wish to build the Church upon these non-Jews as well. Or taking the metaphor even one step deeper: that He also pointed to Himself to remind the apostles not to forget about Him.

Twelve Apostles who were still alive—and who had not done so yet—dispersed once and for all time upon their various evangelist journeys. They were following Jesus's command to spread the Gospel to the rest of the known world. What is known of Peter's travels, his martyrdom, and the final resting place of his earthly remains (as will be the case for all of the other eleven apostles) I will base on:

• Local tradition (a concept mostly ignored by scholars)
• The writings of the early Church Fathers
• Hints from Peter's Epistles and the Gospel of Mark

- The founding traditions of various Christian denominations
- The lack of competing traditions (an idea equally dismissed by scholars)

The Apostolic Council

The Apostolic Council (also known as the Jerusalem Council) took place around 50 AD in the city of Jerusalem. Attendees that we can be sure of that were in attendance were Paul, the apostles Peter and James the Lesser, and possibly John. The meeting's primary purpose was to determine just how much of existing Jewish Mosaic Law that those Gentiles who wished to join the new Christian movement would need to follow. The biggest issue was to decide whether or not new non-Jewish men who wanted to join would need to be circumcised first. It was determined that they did not.

Peter's Travels

Due north of Jerusalem and located in what is today southern Turkey, is the city of Antakya. In the days of the Twelve Apostles, however, the city was called Antioch. At the time, the city was one of the largest in the Roman Empire. It was in Antioch that the term "Christian" first came into common use.

The ancient Church fathers say that it was in Antioch that the apostle Peter (along with Paul) founded a Church and that Peter spent seven years as her first bishop. To this very day, the patriarchs of the Syriac Orthodox Church trace an unbroken line of apostolic authority all the way back to St. Peter. And, quite famously, the city was the location of the "Incident at Antioch." According to St. Paul's Epistle to the Galatians (2:11) it was here that Paul rebuked Peter for treating Gentile converts as inferior to Jewish Christians.

The author of the New Testament book Peter 1 addresses the "exiles of the dispersion in Pontus, Galatia, Cappadocia, Asia, and Bithynia." The third-century Church father, Hippolytus of Rome, confirms Peter's actual visits to these places. If you look at a map of these former Roman provinces that today make up the vast majority of the modern nation of Turkey, it would seem logical as well. Geographically speaking, Peter would have had to pass through these regions on his way to the eastern seaport city of Ephesus. It would have been neglectful of him not to have at least stopped to visit his fellow apostle, John, to say hello and spend the night.

It was from Ephesus that he probably departed for Corinth, a city 180 miles away by sea that still can be visited today in modern Greece. Acts 18:1–17 says that Paul founded the Church in Corinth. However, the first-century bishop of Corinth also included the apostle Peter as a cofounder of the Church: "You have thus by such an admonition bound together the planting of Peter and of Paul at Rome and Corinth. For both of them planted and likewise taught us in our Corinth."

After a short stay in Corinth, the apostle Peter ultimately sailed to Rome and to his martyrdom. Although the matter is slightly controversial, it is very likely that there was already a

thriving Church in the city when Peter arrived there shortly after 62 AD, and that this Church was originally founded by

Paul. Most scholars place the time of his martyrdom—along with Paul's—to have been under the reign of Nero around the year
64 AD. The New Testament is silent on the matter of Peter being crucified in Rome, but the apocryphal literature associated with him overwhelmingly reaffirms the tradition, as do all of the early Church fathers.

For example, in the apocryphal Acts of Peter, the document describes a rather amusing battle of magic powers between Simon Magus and Peter that mentions the Roman Forum. Also, Ignatius, the third bishop of Antioch and an actual student of the apostle John, speaks in one of his letters of Peter and Paul admonishing the Roman Christians. Another early Church Father, Irenaeus of Lyons, whose teacher, Polycarp, the bishop of Smyrna (also a disciple of the apostle John), wrote that Peter and Paul had been the founders of the Church in Rome. In summary, the fact that the apostle Peter was martyred in Rome sometime around the year 64 AD is something that nearly all historians and religious scholars are in complete agreement with. But one of the most important concepts that is available to thinking people—but one that very few academic researchers give much credit to—is that of a lack of any other competing tradition(s).

That is, we have a man, a very important man, a relatively well-known man who, through his dedication and sacrifice, was instrumental in helping to change the course of history. If there was anyplace other than Rome that thinks or feels it has a claim to Peter's martyrdom and burial site, they would be shouting it from the mountaintop. (There's a lot of money to be made from being a pilgrim site, and the world would certainly have heard of it.) Yes, I know there have been a few naysayers out there over the centuries whose bizarre logic and self-serving arguments are in the literature. I have read many of their claims, but on close and objective analysis, the evidence just isn't there.

The Early Church Fathers

The Early Church Fathers were theologians and historians who, through their writings and examples, nurtured and influenced the development of the early Christian Church after the deaths of Jesus and the Twelve Apostles. The study of these ancient Church Fathers is called patristics. Scholars who study patristics traditionally end this period of the early Church at 700 AD. To be considered a Father of the Church requires four qualifications: Antiquity, personal sanctity, proper orthodox belief, and approval of the Church.

— There are several ways patristic scholars have attempted to classify the various groups of Church Fathers and there is great overlap between these categories.

• The Apostolic Fathers were men who actually personally knew one or more of the Twelve Apostles, the Seventy Disciples, or were strongly influenced by them. Examples are Clement of Rome, Ignatius of Antioch and Polycarp of Smyrna.

• The Greek Church Fathers were Irenaeus of Lyons, Clement and Origin of Alexandria, John Chrysostom, and Basil the Great.

• The Latin Fathers were early Christian theologians who wrote in Latin. Examples include Tertullian, Ambrose of Milan, Jerome of Stridonium, Augustine of Hippo.

• Syriac Fathers. These were early Christian theologians who wrote in Syriac, a language spoken throughout the Middle East. Examples include Aphrahat of Mesopotamia and Isaac of Antioch.

• The Desert Fathers were Egyptian monastics whose writings were few but whose influence was great. Examples include Anthony, Pachomius of Thebes and Paul the Anchorite.

— The Catholic and Eastern Orthodox tradition also recognizes the Great Church Fathers. In Catholicism, they are also referred to as the original Doctors of the Church. These are theologians who had a huge influence on early Church doctrine and growth. Examples include Ambrose, Jerome, Augustine, Gregory the Great, Basil the Great, Athanasius, Gregory of Nazianzus, and John Chrysostom.

Visiting St. Peter's Martyrdom Site and Grave

Of all of the Twelve Apostles of Jesus, the site of Peter's martyrdom and the location of his final tomb are the easiest to visit. The only effort involved is making a trip to Rome, Italy, to the Vatican and St. Peter's Basilica. Whether your religious beliefs agree with the primacy of the pope as the Bishop of Rome and the unbroken, apostolic descendant of St. Peter (as do Roman and Eastern Catholics), or whether you disagree (as do the Orthodox and Assyrian Churches and many Protestant sects), everyone is welcome to visit this undisputed tomb of the "Fisher of Men."

To visit the site of St. Peter's martyrdom, you walk to the south transept of the basilica to the Altar of St. Joseph. On the left-hand side of the chapel is the Altar of the Crucifixion. When you stand or kneel in front of the mosaic reproduction of the picture of St. Peter being crucified upside down, you are standing exactly over the center of the ancient Roman Circus Maximus where the apostle died.

The Crucifixion of Peter
By Guido Reni

One of the most distinctive features of St. Peter's Basilica, both from the inside and outside, is its magnificent dome. If you were to shine a laser beam straight down from its midpoint, the light would pass directly through the center of the church's main altar into the grotto below. There it would pass through the remains of the third-century church built by Constantine, which he had constructed directly over the grave of the apostle Peter. When you stand in the crypt below the main floor of the church, outside of a well-marked walled-off area, you will be in the presence of the man that Jesus called Petros, the Rock: a simple Jewish fisherman who walked upon the earth with the Son of Mary, who broke bread with Him at the Last Supper, who loved Him but who also denied his beloved friend three times, who was to witness the Lord's empty tomb, and who would ultimately become the rock upon which Jesus said, "I will build my Church."

It was there in the crypt below St. Peter's Basilica in front of the mortal remains of the great apostle that I stood, laid my hand on the glass wall that separated us, and became "one" with this great man of God. After several minutes of giving him thanks, I continued to just stand there for a couple of minutes in silent awe. It was also at this time that I first asked myself the question, "Rich, I wonder where the rest of these guys are?"

Quo Vadis

Church of Domine Quo Vadis, Rome, Italy
Shutterstock

Two miles southeast of the Vatican along the old Roman Appian Way is the Church of St. Mary in Palmis, better known as the Church of Domine Quo Vadis. The small, ancient church is built over the spot where the apocryphal Acts of Peter state that the apostle Peter met the crucified Christ.

According to the legend, Peter had been captured and sentenced to death by Emperor Nero. His followers, anxious to see him live, broke him out of prison. In one last act of human weakness, the apostle then fled Rome, heading south on the old Roman road. As he reached the spot where the church now stands, he saw his dear old friend and Lord walking toward the city. He asked Jesus, "Domine, quo vadis?"

Where are you going Lord? Tenderly, but tired, and probably once again exasperated by His friend's lapse of faith, Jesus answered, "I am going to Rome to be crucified yet one more time." Moved by his Lord's willingness to suffer once more, Peter regained his courage and said, "Lord, I will return and will follow Thee." Jesus then disappeared, and Peter went back to Rome and to his martyrdom.

The Apostle Simon and His Tool of Martyrdom
Sculpted by Hermann Schievelbein

Chapter Two
The Apostle Simon

ﾂ2ﾘｽ

"When the day of Pentecost came, they were all together in one place." Acts 2:1 NIV

Not too much is known from the New Testament about the apostle Simon. The only times he's mentioned in the Synoptic Gospels of Mark, Luke, and Matthew and Acts is when the evangelist lists the names of the Twelve Apostles.
• Matthew 10:2–4: "These are the names of the twelve apostles: Simon (who is called Peter) and his brother Andrew; James son of Zebedee, and his brother John; Philip and Bartholomew; Thomas and Matthew the tax collector; James son of Alphaeus, and Thaddaeus; Simon the Zealot and Judas Iscariot, who betrayed him."
• Acts 1:12–13: "Then the apostles returned to Jerusalem from the hill called the Mount of Olives, a Sabbath day's walk from the city. When they arrived, they went upstairs to the room where they were staying. Those present were Peter, John, James and Andrew; Philip and Thomas, Bartholomew and Matthew; James son of Alphaeus and Simon the Zealot, and Judas son of James."

Even in these simple lists, there is some mild confusion. The NIV versions of the above lists simplify the matter somewhat by consistently naming him Simon the Zealot. Historically, however, depending on which New Testament translation one reads, his name has also been listed as:
• Simon Kananaios
• Simon Kananites
• Simon the Cananean
• Simon Zealotes

Because of these various names, over the centuries it was assumed that the apostle Simon was from Cana, the biblical site of the wedding feast where Jesus turned the water into wine. Exaggerated versions of the wedding-at-Cana story even have Simon as the groom of the wedding! Language experts, however, now say that the words Kananaios and Kananites both derive from the Hebrew word *qana* (kana), which means "zealot."

There is even confusion over the designation *zealot*. First of all it was important for the New Testament authors to differentiate between the two apostles named Simon. Simon Peter, of course, became simply known as Peter, and the second Simon became Simon the Zealot. It is unclear in the Gospels and Acts why the authors chose the term *zealot*. The easy answer most people like is that he was a member of a group of Jewish revolutionaries who were intent on ridding the Holy Land of their Roman occupiers. A relatively recent interpretation of the word suggests that the apostle was given the nickname because it reflected his zeal for the good news being shared by his friend and teacher, Jesus.

What is known of Simon is, of course, that he was chosen by Jesus at some time during His ministry to be one of his original Twelve Apostles. How or why matters not; Jesus saw something in Simon that made him special. He would then go on to be a firsthand witness to His healing miracles and Resurrection. He would have heard the Sermon on the Mount and would have been there personally to partake in the Miracle of the Loaves and Fishes. He would have consumed the sanctified bread and wine at the Last Supper, then accompanied the Lord to His agony at Gethsemane, and then left Him (like Peter) to suffer His Passion alone. But he redeemed himself — as did all of the other apostles (except Judas Iscariot) — after Pentecost, by spreading the Gospel to the ends of the earth.

The Apostle of Georgia

Where the apostle Simon went after receiving the Holy Spirit at Pentecost is a matter of confusing and improbable speculation. One odd (in my opinion) but not impossible tradition is that the apostle accompanied Joseph of Arimathea to the British Isles after the crucifixion of Jesus. I say it's not impossible because one of the legends as to why Joseph was a "rich man" is that he was involved with the ancient Roman tin trade. This already 1,000-year-old trade in tin, which was mentioned in the Old Testament, made traveling in those days to the British Isles from Rome and Israel a relatively routine event.

Joseph of Arimathea

- Although mentioned in all four Gospels, very little is known with certainty of the life of Joseph of Arimathea. In the Gospels, his biggest claim to fame is that he was a rich man, a member of the Jewish Sanhedrin in Jerusalem, who then had the courage to ask Pontius Pilate for the body of the crucified Jesus. After personally helping Nicodemus remove Him from the Cross, he donated his personal tomb for the Lord's burial.

- From traditional documents and legends, Joseph was a rich man because he was involved in the mining of tin. There's good evidence that as a businessman he regularly traveled to Roman Gaul and England. One ancient text has him as the uncle of Jesus who actually took his nephew with him on one or more trips. After the death of the apostle James the Greater, with its subsequent persecutions, it is likely he traveled to Gaul (modern-day France) with the apostle Philip, Mary Zebedee, Mary Magdalene, and Mary, the mother of James the Less. There is a tradition that he also guided Simon on the apostle's quick mission to England and that Joseph founded a church in what is today the city of Glastonbury. He ultimately died and was buried there. Until recently killed by a madman, there was also a tree that grew in the churchyard that supposedly had sprung forth from Joseph's walking staff. He is credited with bringing the Holy Grail (the cup used at the last supper and in which Joseph collected some of Jesus's blood at His crucifixion) to England, where it then became intertwined with the King Arthur legend!

- Equally uncertain is where exactly Arimathea is located. The prevailing opinion is that the word *Arimathea* is a derivative of the biblical place name Ramathaim-zophim. This town was the home of Elkanah and Hannah and the birthplace of their son, the prophet Samuel. Although not the only contender for the location of Arimathea, the modern-day town of Beit Rima, sixty miles northwest of Jerusalem, seems to satisfy most scholars.

The trouble is that other than a few eleventh-century sources, there are absolutely no local traditions to the apostle Simon being in Britain. And by this I mean that there is no one church or community or pilgrimage site that makes any claim to having been visited by or contains any of the mortal remains of him. Even the Venerable Bede, a seventh-century British monk and historian, doesn't mention Simon being anywhere in the British Isles. More importantly, however, most ancient sources almost unanimously have him preaching in the East: Persia, Armenia, the Republic of Georgia, and the Black Sea region of Colchis. They often have him in the company of the apostle Jude, which adds an extra element of confusion to Simon's story.

One place that always comes up in my researches is a place called Suanir in ancient Persia—a place that doesn't seem to exist either in antiquity or today. It's like somebody wrote the word down in some article a few hundred years ago, and everyone since has mindlessly been copying it. One possibility is they are mistaking it for a place in western Iran called Sufian, which is possibly the location of where the apostle Jude was martyred. However, while I was researching this possible clue— and every other mention of any other place that the apostle Simon may have may reliably visited—I came across the statement made by a fifth-century Armenian historian named Moses of Chorene.

Also known as Movses Khorenatsi, this Moses of Chorene wrote that the apostle Simon was martyred by Roman soldiers at a place called Weriosphora in Caucasian Iberia. At first, this was a bit confusing. When I saw the word *Iberia*, I instantly thought of the Iberian Peninsula, which is the location of the modern-day country of Spain. But upon further investigation, I discovered that Caucasian Iberia was the ancient Greek term for the old kingdom of Georgia. Historically, this was land between the Caspian Sea and the eastern Black Sea, whose most prominent geologic feature is the Caucasus Mountains.

Weriosphora is the region of the ancient kingdom of Georgia that is presently known as the Republic of Abkhazia. A very strong local tradition says that it was here, about twenty miles north of the modern-day city of Sukhum (also called Sebastopolis), that the apostle Simon preached the Gospel for the last ten years of his life. It was here in 55 AD, during the Roman persecution, that he was martyred for his faith and was originally buried.

Abkhazia

- Abkhazia is one of two breakaway republics from the eastern Black Sea nation of Georgia. After a brutal civil war, Abkhazia declared its independence from Georgia in 1999. The border with Russia is just five miles from where the Olympics were held in Sochi.
- The entire region of Abkhazia and western Georgia was known to the ancient Greeks as the Kingdom of Colchis and was home to the legend of Jason and the Argonauts, King Aeëtes and his daughter Medea, and the Golden Fleece.
- The country is in the top three of the entire world with regards to long life spans. As late as the 1970s, Abkhazian citizens were still living to 150 years old with men still fathering children at age 136. There are several theories as to why. One possibility is the water that flows down from the Caucasus Mountains. The other is the wine and vegetables that grow abundantly in the rich soils of the region. Another is their large consumption of fermented dairy products, yogurts, and native cheeses.
- Joseph Stalin and Nikita Khrushchev had summer homes in Abkhazia.
- Abkhazia exports more than 1,500 tons of honey every year.

As part of my quest to research and to visit the places associated with the martyrdoms, the original tombs, as well as the final resting places of the Twelve Apostles of Jesus, I came to the conclusion that I would have to visit the Republic of Abkhazia. It turned out to be easier said than done. This is because the country had just come out of a brutal civil war in its attempt to win its freedom from the Republic of Georgia. As I write this book, Georgia still considers Abkhazia a breakaway republic.

Just before the recent Olympics in Sochi, Russia, I was able to find a tour agency in Abkhazia to issue us visas to enter the country. But before we could do that, we had to obtain double-entry visas to enter Russia, not an easy task. Once doing so, we flew to Sochi, a resort city on the eastern coast of the

Highway to New Athos

Black Sea. Here we connected with a driver and guide and then drove the twenty miles from our hotel to the Russian/Abkhazian border.

Abkhazia turned out to be quite an amazing experience in its own right. Because its beaches and mountain resorts had been the favorites of upper-class Russians for years, the roads and basic infrastructure—at least those not destroyed in the recent civil war—were well- built and cared for. However, it was like going back fifty years in time: horse-driven carts were common, and cattle frequently blocked the road.

After about an hour's drive, we came to the huge Greek Orthodox monastery of St. Simon in an area called New Athos. With her

St. Simon Monastery, New Athos

glistening white onion-shaped domes shining in the afternoon sun, she looked like something from a Dr. Zhivago movie.

After a quick exploration of the monastery complex, our

driver and guide took us to the base of the hill upon which the monastery was built, to the tiny white Orthodox Church of St. Simon the Canaanite. The first church was built upon this site in

St. Simon the Zealot Church: Note the Area Near the Right Wall

the third-century. It was here that the apostle Simon was first buried by his converts and students after his martyrdom. And wouldn't you know it . . . grrrr . . . after all of the work and aggravation involved in getting there, it was locked shut and closed for (according to a passing monk) renovations. However, according to our driver, there was an earthen square on the western side of the building that used to be the original altar area. And it was here that the original grave of St. Simon was located. This bit of information gave me the ability to not only see and photograph the apostle's original burial place, but it allowed me to stand upon the sacred ground as well.

As would be a tradition in each instance of my quests, I knelt down upon the bare, stony earth and gave St. Simon thanks for his great work on behalf of our Lord. After becoming one with another of our Lord's apostles, our guide said it was time to move on to the cave where tradition says he had lived for the last ten years of his life. It was here also that he hid from Emperor Diocletian's Roman legionnaires who had been sent to kill him and all of his Christian converts. She would also show us the exact spot where he was martyred.

Original Burial Location of St. Simon

As we walked past the lake and the man-made waterfalls that were part of a hydroelectric plant and continued along the shore of the Psyrdzhi River, I realized I was now part of a larger pilgrimage tradition celebrated by the Eastern Orthodox and Armenian Christians for over a thousand years. To this day, they refer to Simon the Canaanite as the "Enlightener of Abkhazia" and one of four apostles from whom they trace their apostolic authority. (The others are the apostles Jude, Bartholomew, and Andrew.) Even on this weekday afternoon, there had to be at least a hundred people there.

About a half mile up the now woody trail, we came upon an observation area. Across the river (actually a shallow creek) from this area on the opposite bank was a four-foot-high gray

Martyrdom Site of St. Simon, as Seen From the Trail

granite cross. This cross marks the spot where Simon was martyred. Legend says he met his death by being sawed in half. I wanted to climb over the fence so that I'd be able to lay my hand upon the stone, but our guide said she would show us a spot to cross the

Stairway to St. Simon's Cave

creek on our way back down the trail. We still needed to walk up a big hill to his cave.

So we walked away from the river and up a stone trail carved out of the hill. I have to admit that I puffed a bit and had to stop few times before reaching the mouth of Simon's cave. From my researches—which were

reinforced by our guide—I knew that a tradition of pilgrimage to the cave has been taking place since the first century. After Theresa put on the obligatory head scarf, we walked up the final steps into the cold space of

Interior of Apostle Simon's Cave

the cave, which was illuminated by the lights of several dozen candles. Everywhere we looked there were prayer requests, flowers, and small iconic pictures of the holy apostle. We stayed for several minutes so I could take it all in. Wow!

As promised, on the way back down the trail, the guide showed us a spot where we could crawl through the fence, cross the creek on stepping-stones, and walk back up the other bank to the spot where the brave St. Simon was killed for his faith. I knelt down upon the wet, stony earth and grabbed a handful of soil and just squeezed as hard as I could. There are those who will read this and perhaps will mock me. But I tell you, I could almost feel the hand of the great apostle upon my shoulder, as if to personally let me know all was OK.

Martyrdom Site of St. Simon

Visiting the Final Remains of the Apostle Simon

One question that a gentle reader might be asking at this time is, "Why did you go from talking about the most well-known apostle (Peter) to the least-known (Simon)?" The answer is quite simple, and it has to do with where Simon's final resting place is: If you want to visit the present-day tomb of the apostle Simon, you're already there when you visit the martyrdom site of St. Peter. The main altar in the Chapel of St. Joseph is built right over the crypt containing the earthly remains of Simon. (As an aside, his remains are side by side with those of St. Jude.)

How the apostle's bones arrived there is a complete mystery. After a long search in which I typed in every keyword and followed each possible evidence thread, the only statement I could find regarding the apostle and the Vatican was written by the Brazilian Catholic social activist and philosopher, Professor Plinio Corrêa de Oliveira. He declared, with no further comment: "In 1605, the relics of the two Apostles were transported to the Vatican Basilica and placed in a crypt under the Altar of the Crucifixion."

I do, however, have a couple of theories as to how St. Simon's earthly remains got to the Chapel of St. Joseph, theories that place his remains in their Vatican tomb much, much earlier than 1605. I base these theories on several key points:
• Many of the Twelve Apostles' bones (and the earthly remains of many others of the Christian Church's early saints) were often removed from their original burial sites to prevent their destruction/desecration by the early Muslim conquests.
• Most of the graves located in the lands of Moslem conquest had their remains translated first to the safety of Constantinople, the Patriarchate of the Eastern Church.
• I found multiple references to Holy Roman Emperor Charlemagne donating the apostle's bones to both the Vatican and St. Sernin's Basilica in Toulouse, France.

The first theory involves Emperor Constantine the Great and the original Church of the Holy Apostles in Constantinople. The emperor's intention in 330 AD was to build a church with a tomb that contained himself at the center, surrounded by the Twelve Apostles. I will have more to say on this when I get to the chapter on the apostle Andrew, who historians know for certain was there. But for now, I have found no evidence for

Simon being there.

A more likely possibility is as follows: In 735 AD, the Kingdom of Abkhazia was attacked by a large Muslim army led by a general named Marwan. They laid siege to the city of Anakopia, the ancient name of the city of Novy Afon, where I described previously visiting the original grave and martyrdom site of the apostle Simon. King Leon the First, who ruled Abkhazia at the time, ultimately prevailed in the battle, with the help of his friend, the Byzantine emperor Leo the Third. Anticipating the desecration of the grave of the "Enlightener of Abkhazia," King Leon had the apostle's mortal remains sent to Constantinople for safekeeping.

King Leon's friend, Byzantine emperor Leo the Third, died a short time later in 741. His grandson, Emperor Leo the Forth, married an Athenian woman named Irene. When Irene's husband died, she became regent for her nine-year-old son, Constantine the Sixth. As regent, Irene immediately began to reach out and try to improve relationships with both the papacy in Rome and with the Carolingian dynasty of the soon-to-be Holy Roman Emperor, Charlemagne. She even went so far as to arrange a marriage between her son and Charlemagne's daughter Rotrude. Knowing Charlemagne's devotion to the Western Christian Church, the relics were very likely part of the dowry. In this way, Charlemagne was able to donate these relics to the Vatican and the Basilica of St. Sernin.

A Final Thought

The name Simon comes from the Hebrew word *Shim'on*, which means "he has heard." Perhaps this was his special attribute that appealed to Jesus when he was choosing His special twelve followers. This may have been why the Lord gave him the nickname "The Zealot." Rather than trying to grab the limelight as did Peter and the sons of Zebedee throughout the Gospels, Simon humbly chose instead to listen and learn, literally at the feet of his Master, with an intensity and a zeal that made him stand out among his peers.

I close with a quote that I copied from the website 12.eu/simon. I apologize for not being able to find the name of the author. He/she says: "Simon, the unknown apostle, is the patron of the countless Christians who go through life without fame, without a name. He is the patron of the army of unknown workers in the vineyard of the Lord, who toil in the last places for the kingdom of God. He is the patron of the unknown soldiers of Christ, who struggle on the disregarded and thankless fronts. No one notices, no one praises, no one rewards this obscure and often misunderstood apostle — no one except the Father, who sees through all obscurity, who understands all misjudgments."

The Apostle Andrew's Martyrdom on a Crux Decussata
Detail from a mosaic mural in the Cathedral of St. Andrew, Patras, Greece

Chapter Three
Ꙁᴛʏᴀˢ The Apostle Andrew

Andrew, Simon Peter's brother, was one of the two who heard what John [the Baptist] had said and who had followed Jesus. The first thing Andrew did was to find his brother Simon and tell him, "We have found the Messiah" (that is, the Christ). John 1:40–41 NIV

The apostle Andrew was the brother of Simon Peter. Like his father and brother, he was a fisherman on the Sea of Galilee. Andrew was also a devoted follower of the desert prophet, John the Baptist. One day near the small village of Bethany, as he and John's followers watched the Baptist preaching and baptizing new devotees in the waters of the Jordan River, a young man from Nazareth appeared, wishing to be baptized. John, recognizing his cousin Jesus, hesitated at first; he felt unworthy of such a great honor. But ultimately he did his job and baptized the Lord. And in doing so, he changed the course of history.

After doing so and realizing that his part in the greatest story ever told was now over, the Baptist introduced Andrew to Jesus. Later Church Fathers would forever afterward refer to the apostle Andrew as "the first-called"; the first-called not only of the Twelve Apostles but of the billions of women and men who have accepted Jesus as their savior since that day over 2,000 years ago. It would be only natural that he would want to share the news with his brother, Simon Peter.

From that point on, however, neither the Gospels nor Acts say much about Andrew. It was he who pointed out to Jesus the boy with the five loaves of bread and the five fishes at the Miracle of the Loaves and Fishes. Sometime later, both Andrew and the apostle Phillip introduced Jesus to a pair of unnamed Greeks. Although he is not specifically named, it is very likely that Andrew was with Jesus at Caesarea-Philippi when the Lord told his brother Peter that "on this rock I will build My Church." The fact that he, Andrew, had introduced Peter to Jesus in the first place must have made him feel exceptionally proud.

After Pentecost, and if even only half of the legends regarding Andrew's missionary journeys on behalf of the new Christian Church were true, hands down, he would win the prize of the most traveled of all of the Twelve. Obscure sources have the apostle traveling east and west from Scotland to Kazakhstan and north and south from Russia to Tanzania. One recent author, a Greek investigative reporter named George Alexandrou, has even written a 1,000-page book in which he states that Andrew actually went on four missionary journeys! I've only read excerpts from the book, as it is written in Greek.

In trying to recount Andrew's missionary journey, I will stick to more time-proven and historical sources. I do so not to completely discount the massive work of Mr. Alexandrou but because I believe the time needed for Andrew to have traveled as much as this author claims would make the journeys impossible. (Mr. Alexandrou even has Andrew sojourning in Romania for twenty years!)

The apostle had only twenty-seven years between the time of the first Christian Pentecost in 33 AD to the time of his martyrdom during the reign of Nero in 60 AD. As good as the Roman systems of roads and sea lanes were at the beginning of the first millennium, unless Andrew could fly — and there are no fantastical legends of him having this ability — the journey I share below will be more logical.

Origen of Alexandria (185–232), in his massive writings and commentaries of the early Church, states that Andrew preached in Scythia, a region known to the ancient Greeks that was north of the Black and Caspian Seas that today includes eastern Poland, Ukraine, the Republic of Georgia, southern Russia, and Kazakhstan. The fact that he established churches in this region is supported by the fact that Orthodox churches of both the Georgian Republic and Abkhazia trace their apostolic authority to the apostles Andrew and Simon the Zealot.

The Order of St. Andrew

In *The Chronicles of Nestor*, which is the first written comprehensive history of the eastern Slavic peoples, an Orthodox monk named, of course, Nestor (1056–1114) states that after preaching along the eastern coast of the Black Sea, Andrew sailed northward from modern-day Odessa up the Dnieper River to Kiev, the capital of Ukraine. Further local tradition has the apostle traveling farther north to the region between Moscow and St. Petersburg. To this day, the apostle is the patron saint of Georgia, Ukraine, and Russia.

The Order of St. Andrew the Apostle

In honor of the Patron Saint of Russia, Tsar Peter the Great established the Order of St. Andrew the Apostle in 1689. The award is given to "reward prominent statesmen and public figures, eminent representatives of science, culture, the arts and various industries for exceptional services, for promoting the prosperity, grandeur and glory of Russia." Recent recipients include author Alexander Solzhenitsyn, gun designer Mikhail Kalashnikov, Mikhail Gorbachev, poet Rasul Gamzatov, and dancer and choreographer Yury Grigorovich.

Andrew then traveled southward back to the Black Sea, probably taking one of the ancient Amber Road trade routes down the Vistula River through central Poland and the lower Dnieper. He then sailed south from Chersonesus (near the modern city of Sevastopol) on the Crimean Peninsula across the Black Sea to the port city of Sinope in today's modern Turkey.

Here he probably lingered for a time as tradition says, making side trips to Pontus, Galatia, and Cappadocia. Though there exists no tradition that I could find, the timing and locations would have made it possible that he and his brother Peter, the two sons of Jonah, may have had one last precious visit together before parting forever on their separate paths to eternal glory.

Andrew then traveled westward through the regions of Bithynia and Asia to what was then a small former Greek outpost called Byzantium. There, in what would become the great city of Constantinople (modern-day Istanbul, Turkey), he established a church. There he met up with one of the seventy disciples of Jesus, a man named Stachys. He then installed Stachys as the first bishop of what would eventually become the Patriarchate of Constantinople. To this day, all of the archbishops of Constantinople consider themselves successors of the apostle Andrew. The present ecumenical patriarch, "His Most Divine All-Holiness the Archbishop of Constantinople, New Rome and Ecumenical Patriarch" Bartholomew I, is the 270th holder of the sacred title.

There is a reputable legend that says that on one of these missionary voyages around the southern coast of Turkey, the ship carrying him between ports got lost in a storm and crashed

Apostolos Andreas Monastery

upon the rocky eastern shore of the Island of Cyprus. It is said that the apostle struck a rock with his staff and sweet water emerged that still flows in this parched desert region today. A Greek Orthodox church called the Apostolos Andreas Monastery has been built over the site of the well. A place of great pilgrimage, the monastery fell into disrepair as a result of the Cypriot/Turkish Civil War. The church has only recently been reopened for visitors.

He then moved northwestward through Thrace (modern Bulgaria), to where tradition says he stopped for many years in Roman Dacia (modern-day Romania). After founding many churches, Andrew traveled southward thru Macedonia and Albania, ending up in a city on the west coast of Greece called Patras. It was here in Patras in the year 60 AD that Andrew was martyred after angering the local governor by baptizing his wife, Maximilla, and his brother, Stratokles. Because he considered himself unworthy of the same form of crucifixion as Jesus, the apostle chose to die instead on a *crux decussata*, an X-shaped cross.

Visiting the Site of the Apostle Andrew's Martyrdom

Directly across the street from the Port of Patras, Greece, is a huge Orthodox church called, appropriately, the Cathedral of St. Andrew. The building is the largest Greek Orthodox church in Greece. Just to the left side (south) of the main entrance to this church is a small chapel built over a small spring that in antiquity was dedicated to Demeter, the Greek goddess of the harvest. It is here that the apostle Andrew was said to have preached and where he was ultimately martyred.

We were told by the

guide books that the passage down to the well and martyrdom site was normally locked to pilgrims and visitors. However, just on a whim, after our evening meal, we saw there was a lot of activity going on at the cathedral, so we thought we'd check it out. As luck would have it, whatever the occasion the good people of Patras were celebrating, the entrance to the well was unlocked! And even better, there was no one around to prevent us from exploring in detail the whole subterranean structure.

And so to visit the martyrdom site of the apostle Andrew, all you have to do is walk down the stairs to where you'll find old Demeter's well. Then you turn right, and you'll see a wall with a big saltier cross painted upon it. You will then be in the sacred presence of where legend says the apostle lingered on an X-shaped cross for two days, preaching all the while the Good News of Jesus, before finally joining his friend and Lord in heaven.

Maximilla had the mortal remains of God's first-called buried with honors at the site of his execution near the shore of the Gulf of Patras. There his bones rested for a few hundred years until they began yet another great—a somewhat complicated and confusing journey. The modern-day Greek Orthodox Cathedral of St. Andrew is built over this original, but now empty, tomb.

Visiting the Final Remains of the Apostle Andrew

The simple answer as to where to go today to visit the official final resting place of the apostle Andrew is that all you have to do is travel to the seaside town of Amalfi, Italy. There, in one of the more beautiful areas of the world, in the equally

The Church of St. Andrew, Amalfi, Italy

Tomb of St. Andrew

stunningly beautiful Cathedral of St. Andrew, you can go down into the crypt below the main altar and stand before the padlocked tomb of the first-called apostle. How the apostle got there is quite a fascinating story.

It is also possible to visit two less elaborate shrines devoted to Andrew. This can be done by visiting St. Mary's Roman Catholic Church in Edinburgh, Scotland, and, quite appropriately, the Greek Orthodox Cathedral of St. Andrew in Patras, Greece. How these rather significant fragments of Andrew's bones got to each of these places are interesting stories as well.

Generally speaking — and other than the grave of Peter — the mortal remains of the apostle Andrew have the most historically accurate documentation of any of the relics of the remaining apostles. After his crucifixion and burial in 60 AD, his relics rested peacefully in the western Greek city of Patras. This would all end less than 300 years later when the Roman Emperor Constantine the Great declared Christianity the official religion of the empire.

In the year 330, Constantine conceived of the notion to build a great church for himself in Constantinople to ultimately

serve as his tomb. This church would be called the Church of the Holy Apostles. Because he had "saved" Christianity, the emperor had this opinion of himself as being the thirteenth apostle. His intention was to gather together all

Fatih Mosque, Istanbul, Turkey

of the mortal remains of the Twelve Apostles of Jesus into one place, with his grave being in the center of the group. He died

before the church's completion, however, and his son Constantius the Second finished the job. In 357, per his father's wishes, he had the bones of Andrew translated from Patras to Constantinople. Historians are not in complete agreement as to which other apostles (Philip? James the Less?) were eventually moved to Constantine's new church. All are in agreement, however, that
Andrew was there.

The Church of the Holy Apostles ultimately became the burial site of the next hundreds of years of Constantinople's saints and ruling elites. In 1204, the crusaders of the Forth Crusade plundered and destroyed Constantinople. To protect the mortal remains of Andrew, Cardinal Peter of Capua, the pope's representative to the Eastern Church, managed to

Courtyard of the Fatih Mosque

remove his body and translate the remains to his hometown of Amalfi, in southern Italy, where they sit today in the Cathedral of St. Andrew. Then, after the Muslim conquest in 1453,

Constantine's church fell into disrepair. Today, the equally beautiful and very impressive Fatih Mosque stands on the grounds of the former church. In the garden of this mosque, there are sixteen green stone pillars; these are the only remnant of Constantine's great church.

But There Are Parts B and C to Andrew's Story!

Part B: Around the time that Constantine had the self-serving idea to build his church, a man who would someday become known as St. Regulus had a dream. In his dream, Regulus (who was Bishop of Patras at the time) was told by an angel to remove for safekeeping as many bones of the apostle Andrew as he was able, and to travel with them as far as he could to the western ends of the world. Legend says he managed to obtain three finger bones, a tooth, a kneecap, and a humerus (upper arm bone). As an aside, one report I read of Regulus's journey was that he was accompanied in his mission by a large number of consecrated virgins, including one woman who would later be known as Saint Triduana.

Saint Triduana

Saint Triduana (also known as Trodline, Tredwell, and Trøllhaena) was a Christian nun born in Colossae, Greece, who traveled along with St. Rule (Regulus) and the bones of the apostle Andrew from Constantinople to northern Scotland in the fourth century. Shortly after she arrived in Scotland, her great beauty caught the attention of King Nectans, the ruler of the Picts. Because the king had complimented her on the beauty of her eyes, to prevent his further advances, she plucked them out of their sockets, skewered them onto a sharpened stick, and gave them to Nectan. After her death, she was buried in the parish church in the former village of Restalrig, now part of Edinburgh. To this very day, she is the patron saint of blindness and other eye diseases.

The same angel then told Regulus (also known as St. Rule) to end his journey along the northern shore of the Fife River at a Pictish village called Kilrymont, which today is called St. Andrews. Here, he would found a church dedicated to the

The Ruins of St. Andrew's Cathedral, St. Andrews, Scotland

apostle Andrew. Although it took awhile, the Cathedral of St. Andrew was finally completed in 1058. There it stood as a site of holy pilgrimage until the Scottish Reformation in June 1559. Under the orders of John Knox, the relics of Andrew were then supposedly destroyed in the carnage when the reformers looted the church. I say "supposedly" because, on a visit to the ruined cathedral, I spoke with a local guide who told me that the relics may still be in the wall behind the location of the original main altar marked with an "X!"

As a result of the Reformation, Catholic worship was outlawed in Scotland. In 1878, this ability to worship was restored. Even though Andrew's bones may or may not be any longer in the city of St. Andrews, you can visit some of the apostle's relics in Edinburgh. In 1879, the archbishop of Amalfi sent the newly reinstated St. Mary's Roman Catholic Church a sizable piece of Andrew's scapula (shoulder blade). In honor of the appointment of Cardinal Gordon Joseph Gray, the first Scottish Cardinal in 400 years, Pope Paul the Sixth in 1969 sent another relic to the Shrine of St. Andrew.

Part C: Today, in Patras, Greece, a huge Greek Orthodox church, the Cathedral of St. Andrew, stands over the site of the apostle Andrew's crucifixion and burial. Inside the church, to the right of the main altar, there is a large silver reliquary. When you look inside the glass dome, you can see a large piece of the skull bone of the apostle. How it arrived there is quite amazing as well.

One of the greatest of the old Byzantine Empire's rulers was Emperor Basil the First. Born a commoner, Basil reigned from 867 to 886. For reasons I could not find—perhaps because Basil was born in Macedonia, a country that is today just north of Greece—he returned this piece of Andrew's skull to Patras. There the relic stayed until 1461, when the Turkish Ottomans

invaded the region. The local ruler, Thomas Palaeologus, realizing the Ottomans' propensity to destroy Christian relics, fled in exile to Italy, bringing with him the skull. Thomas Palaeologus gave the skull to Pope

Reliquary Containing Part of the Skull of St. Andrew. To the Left is A Large Portion of His X-shaped Cross.

Pius the Second. The pope then had the skull enshrined in one of the four central piers of St. Peter's Basilica. For the next five hundred years, the bones of the two sons of Jonah were reunited.

However, in 1964, Pope Paul the Sixth ordered that the skull—and all other relics of the apostle that the Vatican owned—were to be returned to the Greek Orthodox church in Patras, where you can see it today.

The Cathedral of St. Andrew, Patras, Greece

The Apostle Bartholomew Holding His Flayed Skin

Chapter Four
The Apostle Bartholomew

"Nazareth! Can anything good come from there?" Nathanael [Bartholomew] asked. "Come and see," said Philip. When Jesus saw Nathanael approaching, he said of him, "Here truly is an Israelite in whom there is no deceit." John 1:46–47 NIV

The Gospel writers Mark, Luke, and Matthew say almost nothing about the apostle Bartholomew. The only time he appears is when these three writers list the Twelve, and then he is always mentioned right after the apostle Philip. What little we do know about Bartholomew is found in the first two verses of John's Gospel. The only confusing part is that John calls him by the name Nathanael.

How or why this is the case has driven both the early Church Fathers and modern-day New Testament scholars crazy. The most accepted answer is that Bartholomew was actually the apostle's last name. According to ancient Jewish tradition, the prefix *bar* meant "son of." Therefore, in this case, his last name would translate as "son of Tolmai." Nathanael was most likely his familiar or first name.

John writes that he was from Cana in Galilee, a small village about ten miles northeast of Nazareth. It was in this small town of Bartholomew's where Jesus performed his first earthly miracle of turning water into wine. The assumption is made, wrongly I believe, that, like Peter, Andrew, John, and James, he was a fisherman. However, his name, son of Tolmai, is interpreted by many as son of the furrower or ploughman, which would make him a farmer.

After being called by Jesus, we can assume that Bartholomew/Nathanael—as part of the Twelve—followed Him on all of His journeys throughout Israel. He was there at the Sermon on the Mount, which would have been just a two-day walk from his hometown of Cana. Like the rest of the Twelve, he was there when the hapless woman who had been bleeding for twelve years reached out to grasp the edge of Jesus's cloak, inspiring Him to ask the question, "Who touched me?" Luke 8:43–48 NIV. And Bartholomew was there at Pentecost where he received the Holy Ghost and the commission to spread the Gospel thoughout the known world.

St. Bartholomew's missionary journeys after Pentecost can only be described as a chaos of contradictions, misunderstandings, and historical confusion with regards to ancient geography. One possibility is that Bartholomew's missionary journey to India was confused and/or commingled with that of the apostle Thomas, the official apostle of India. A good example of the confusion regarding the state of world geography of his time concerns precisely what the early Church Fathers meant when they spoke of India. One of the first historians of the early Church, Hippolytus of Rome (170–235), wrote that "Bartholomew preached to the Indians." Eusebius of Caesarea and St. Jerome both tell the story of a second-century missionary to India named Pantaenus of Alexandria who discovered when he got there that the local people had already been preached to by Bartholomew.

The problem with this statement is that the Church historians of those early centuries used the term "India" rather casually. For some writers the word actually was intended to mean the modern-day, subcontinent country we call India. For others, India was a term describing the broad region of the world east of the Euphrates River, with the Arabian Peninsula and the region of modern Ethiopia thrown into the mix as well. And so the question of whether or not the apostle Bartholomew made it to modern-day India is still being debated. Modern scholarship and my extensive researches suggest that he did indeed make it there.

Regardless of whether he participated in the evangelizing of India or not, all religious scholars are in agreement that he was strictly an apostle to the Eastern Churches, especially to that of Armenia, where he was eventually martyred. The ancient writers also have him preaching in Ethiopia, Parthia (northern Iran), Mesopotamia, Lycaonia (central Turkey), Persia, Egypt, Armenia, Arabia, and along the shores of the Black Sea. Although no one will ever know with absolute certainty the exact extent of Bartholomew's journeys, I believe from my research of these many ancient traditions that it's possible he visited all of them.

From the time of Pentecost to the date of his death in 70 AD, Bartholomew would have had thirty-three years to achieve this mission. Using the many existing Roman roads, camel caravan trails, and well-charted sea routes, this all could have been accomplished in this time frame. Although his journeys may not have been without personal deprivation and great personal risk, all along these various routes would have been synagogues, trading stations, large cities, and thriving seaports.

Frankincense Tree in Oman

The earliest date I could uncover of Bartholomew's missionary journeys was his arrival onto the Indian subcontinent in 55 AD, which was twenty-two years after Pentecost. After receiving his commission to spread the Gospel and traveling southward from Jerusalem along the ancient frankincense trade routes, the apostle very possibly traveled through the former Nabatean kingdom, whose capital city of Petra is located in present-day southern Jordan. From there he either sailed down the Gulf of Aqaba into the Red Sea or took the camel caravan routes that stopped in cities today known as Medina and Mecca on down to the area known by the Romans as Arabia Felix, the modern-day countries of Yemen and Oman. In those days — as it is to this very day — this was the center of the cultivation of the trees that produce frankincense.

Here was the kingdom of Aksum, the traditional home of the Queen of Sheba. This kingdom at one time rivaled that of Egypt and Rome and is located today in northeast Ethiopia and Yemen. The kingdom's fortune derived strictly from their control of the southern entrance to the Red Sea, giving them both control of the frankincense trade and the spice trade from India and

Southeast Asia. Here the

Queen of Sheba's Palace, Aksum, Ethiopia

apostle may have sojourned for awhile, giving proof of what the ancient Church Fathers claim as to his preaching in Ethiopia and Arabia. Here he lingered, probably in the seaport of Aden, until the April/September trade winds became favorable to his crossing the Erythraean Sea (today known as the Indian Ocean) on a well-traveled voyage to the subcontinent of India.

Tradition says Bartholomew landed on the central western coast of India in 55 AD in the region today known as Mumbai (Bombay). Here, according to local tradition, he sailed thirty miles up the Ulhas River and preached to the inhabitants of the present-day city of Kalyan. It is stated by the early Church Fathers, Eusebius of Caesarea and St. Jerome, that the apostle left behind him a copy of the Gospel of Matthew. Recent scholarship by Indian researchers seems to verify Bartholomew's short sojourn in their country.

The next mention of St. Bartholomew is of him preaching along with the apostle Philip in the kingdoms of Phrygia and Lydia (modern-day central western Turkey). This would have been possible by traveling either the land or sea spice routes westward across the Arabian Sea, up the Gulf of Oman, and through the Straits of Hormuz into the Persian Gulf. Here, according to the non-canonical book, the Acts of Philip, local tradition says they both were crucified in the city of Hierapolis (modern-day Pamuukale) around the year 62 AD. Local legend says that the preaching of the apostle Philip was so convincing that the local governor removed Bartholomew from his cross and let him go.

Bartholomew's final story has him joining forces for a short while with the apostle Thaddaeus (St. Jude) in the ancient kingdom of Armenia. To this very day, the Armenian Orthodox Church traces their apostolic authority to both of these holy men. Still then within the Armenian Kingdom, history has him traveling to the west shore of the Caspian Sea. There in the

Ruins of St. Bartholomew's Church, Baku, Azerbaijan

modern-day country of Azerbaijan, in the city of Baku, he built a church. The ruins of this church are located right at the base of the Maiden Tower and have recently been excavated.

It is here in the former kingdom of Armenia (not to be

confused with the former Soviet Union Republic of Armenia) that the vast majority of both the early Church Fathers and modern scholarship arrive at some sort of agreement with regards to the martyrdom of Bartholomew.

Around the years 70 and 71 AD, the apostle arrived in the region that was then at the heart of the ancient kingdom of Armenia, the part of the world that today includes southeastern Turkey, northeastern Iraq, and northwestern Iran. Here the Armenian Church says he converted many souls to Jesus Christ, including a person named Princess Vokouhi, daughter of the king, Sanadroug, on a hill just a few miles east of the modern-day Turkish city of Baskale, just ten miles from the border with Iran. Upon hearing of his sister's conversion to Christianity, King Sanadroug then ordered Bartholomew's death by having him flayed (skinned) alive and then beheading him. In the first century, a great monastery was founded upon the site of his death and burial. Ruins of this great church still exist to this day.

Visiting the site of Bartholomew's martyrdom was, and still is, the most difficult of all our apostle quests. Prior to 2013, due to Baskale's proximity to both the borders of Iran and Iraq, the Monastery of St. Bartholomew had the bad luck (at least to a prospective visitor's point of view) of finding itself located right in the middle of a Turkish Army base. The area also had a lot of troubles involving the Kurdish insurgencies. These unfortunate quirks in geopolitics made the monastery completely off limits to researchers and photographers. On the whole of the World Wide Web, I was able to find only two photographs of the former church: One taken in the early 1900s and the other taken in the 1960s.

Anxious to accomplish this goal of at least seeing the building and getting a feel for the essence of its location, I managed to find a tourist agency in London who said they could provide me with a local driver willing to drive us there. We then flew to the western Turkish city of Van. Located on the eastern shore of Lake Van, the city is one of the oldest in the world, with some legends saying that it was originally founded

Monastery of St. Bartholomew, Baskale, Turkey

Main Altar of St. Bartholomew's Church with Cave Entrance to the Right

by the descendants of Noah.

The next day we met our driver who firmly laid down the rules. First of all, he made sure we would not take any photographs. He told us that the best he would possibly be able to do was to take us to a hillside location a few miles from the army base where we could look over to the monastery. I agreed to his terms, and we then drove the two-hour drive to Baskale. When we arrived near the area of the church, we had to pass through an army checkpoint.

Monastery of St. Bartholomew
Baskale, Turkey

It was here that we learned—almost miraculously—that, due to a recent peace accord with the Kurds, the soldiers had pulled their forces off the base and that now we could do whatever we wanted! We then drove the last ten miles to the former army base and indeed, the barbed wire had been pulled away and we could walk up the hill to the ruins of the old church.

We then walked around taking hundreds of photographs and videos of the fallen-down building, trying to figure out where the main altar was. As luck would have it, again, an "angel" (for lack of a better term) showed up to help us. A very ancient Kurdish shepherd extremely curious as to what we were doing came to us, with his fifteen or so sheep, and began speaking with our driver. It turns out we were the first Westerners he'd seen in the area in fifty years! Because the church was still intact when he was a boy, he said that he also knew where everything was and that he was willing to show us.

Thanks to this kind man, I can share the details for use by future visitors. When you enter the church, you walk over the rubble of the fallen dome (toward the north) as far as you can, and you will be standing in front of the main altar. It was on this spot that the apostle Bartholomew was martyred and was originally buried. The shepherd told us that to the right (east) of the alcove was a stairway — now filled with rubble — that led to a cave that Bartholomew lived in the last years of his life. He then gently grabbed hold of my shirt sleeve and walked me over to the back side of the former altar. There he very reverently pointed out dozens of wax stains from the burning of candles in several of the rock niches near the wall of the altar.

Our friend then had to leave. I offered him a small financial token of our appreciation, but he declined. The driver said that he would be happy with a simple handshake. As quick as he appeared, the shepherd and his sheep were gone. When I was alone, I silently stood there (as is my wont) and bonded spiritually with the great man of God. He suffered in his last hours on earth more than any of the other apostles, and I just wanted to thank him for his devotion to the Lord on our behalf.

As an aside, it was while doing research a few years later on the region of Baskale that I learned this was the heart of the ancient Kingdom of Armenia (again, not to be confused with the modern-day nation of Armenia). Having taken their apostolic authority from both Bartholomew and Jude Thaddaeus, technically, when a member of the Armenian Church visited the Monastery of St. Bartholomew, it was an identical experience to me, as a Catholic Christian, visiting the Vatican. I also learned that this region of Turkey was also at the heart of the extremely controversial Armenian Genocide (1915–1918.) As a lover of both the countries of Turkey and Armenia, and because as a general rule I hate all politics, that is all I'm going to say on the matter.

The sad fact of all this, however, is that not one ethnic Armenian is left in the vicinity of St. Bartholomew's Church. The Armenians have also been forbidden for almost one hundred years from worshiping at their Mother Church. It then dawned upon me when I read this that it was probably for this reason that the Kurdish shepherd made it a point to show me the wax stains on the altar. The great monastery was becoming once again a living House of God.

The Apostle Bartholomew's Remains Today

Like many of the other Twelve Apostles, the journey of Bartholomew's earthly remains has several confusing twists and turns. The first translation of the apostle's remains was carried out by the Byzantine emperor Anastasius the First around 507 AD. Most reference sources state that the city to which he moved them was Dura-Europos, a former Roman city in east central Syria. These many authors are incorrect. Dura-Europos was abandoned after a Sassanian siege in the year 257 and has remained untouched until modern times.

The proper location of Emperor Anastasius's city was the city of Dara Mesopotamia, the ruins of which are located in southern Turkey near the border with Syria. Conveniently, the city was only two hundred miles from Bartholomew's original burial site. Beginning in the year 505, the emperor began fortifying this former small village to support the Byzantine Empire's war with the Persians and Saracens. Among all of the new walls and storehouses and public baths, workers built a great church dedicated to St. Bartholomew.

It was in this church that the apostle's relics rested until just before the city was captured by the Persians. Bartholomew's remains next showed up with certainty on Lipari, a small island off the north coast of Sicily. The existence of these relics can be traced back to the year 546. How they got there is still a matter of speculation. St. Gregory of Tours speaks of Bartholomew's remains washing up upon the shore of the island in a lead-sealed coffin. Although this is a good story, it's more likely — because the island was still under control of the

Byzantine Empire at the time—they were brought there by an unknown pious traveler or trader who rescued them from the fallen Dara Mesopotamia. Adding great validity to Lipari's claim to having been guardian of Bartholomew's remains is that a picture of the apostle holding his flayed skin still adorns Lipari's coat of arms.

In the year 836, Saracen pirates attacked Lipari and killed the vast majority of the population. Bartholomew's remains were rescued by a Lombard prince named Sicardo, with the help of hired Amalfian merchants, and then taken to the Italian mainland city of Benevento. In 983, after conquering the city, Holy Roman Emperor Otto II had the apostle's remains transferred to Rome. Otto's intentions were to then have the remains sent to

Skull of St. Bartholomew
Frankfort Cathedral

Germany. However, while he was in Rome supervising the election of a new pope, he contracted malaria and died. But not before having a large piece of the apostle's skull sent to the city of Frankfurt, where it can be seen today.

In the year 998 his son, Otto III, began work upon a new church on an island in the Tiber River, which today is called the Basilica of San Bartolomeo all'Isola. Interestingly, the church was built upon the foundation of a former temple dedicated to the Greek god of medicine, Aesculapius. It is there under the main altar of the church in what looks like a large, red granite bathtub, that the vast majority of the apostle's mortal remains—including his flayed skin—are enshrined. As an aside, of all of the Twelve Apostles' final resting places, Bartholomew's tomb is the only one that a visitor/pilgrim can actually touch (without incurring the wrath of a devoted nun or church caretaker).

Basilica of St. Bartholomew, Rome, Italy
Shutterstock Images

Final Resting Place of the Apostle Bartholomew

Addendum:

St. Bartholomew is the patron saint of medical doctors and, oddly, the saint of mental and nervous disorders. This may be due to the fact that the present-day location of his tomb was an ancient Greek temple dedicated to the god of medicine, Aesculapius. The apostle is also known for miracles involving weights and measures. One of the more famous of these occurred on the island of Lipari where his mortal remains had rested for about three hundred years.

During the Fascist occupation of the island during World War Two, Italian soldiers raided St. Bartholomew's Church and seized a silver statue of the apostle. Looking to melt it down to help Mussolini pay for the war effort, the soldiers discovered when they weighed the statue that it only weighed a few ounces. Because it was such an insignificant amount, they returned it to the church. After the war, during the Feast of St. Bartholomew, when the statue was removed from its location near the main altar of the church, it was discovered to weigh over one hundred pounds and needed four men to carry it on its procession through town.

The Apostle Jude Thaddeaus Holding the Image of Jesus
Shutterstock Images

Chapter Five
The Apostle Jude

2 1/2 YRS

Then Judas (not Judas Iscariot) said, "But, Lord, why do you intend to show yourself to us and not to the world?" John 14:22 NIV

With this relatively innocent and short question, the apostle Jude (not Iscariot) forever has the distinction of being the last of the Lord's Twelve Apostles to ask the living, not-yet-resurrected Jesus a question. Also within the context of this New Testament passage is a dilemma that all of the early Church Fathers, and all of the biblical commentators of the Gospels and of the Acts of the Apostles since those ancient days have had to contend with: that of confusing Jude (Judas in Greek), the apostle who went on to spread the good news of Jesus to the world with that of Judas Iscariot, the apostle who betrayed the Lord.

Recognizing that this possibility existed, the Gospel writers themselves did their best to make the distinction clear. In their lists of the Twelve Apostles, both Matthew and Mark refer to him as Thaddaeus. Luke lists his name as Judas, son of James. To confuse the situation even further, there exist a few New Testament translations where Matthew refers to the apostle Jude as Lebbaeus, whose surname was Thaddaeus. As an aside, this Thaddaeus/Lebbaeus quandary is quite easy to understand. Thaddaeus is a derivation of the Aramaic word *tad*, meaning "breast." Lebbaeus is derived from the Hebrew word for "heart." Both words refer to someone who is loved by the person speaking his name.

Other than the brief question that he asked Jesus during the Last Supper and his listing in all of the four Gospels (and Acts) of the Twelve Apostles, nothing else is said about Jude.

Other than the Western Church's tradition of celebrating him as being the "saint of lost causes," nothing else is known about him. However, within the realm of the Eastern Church, especially that of the Armenian Church, there is a huge amount of written documents and oral history regarding the apostle. As a matter of fact, they derive not only their founding by the apostles Thaddaeus (they prefer the name Thaddaeus instead of Jude) and Bartholomew, but their apostolic authority as well. The Assyrian Church of the East, the Chaldean Catholic Church, the Chaldean Syrian Church, and the Syro-Malabar Catholic Church in India also claim a connection to this apostle.

The Great Schism

• Although it was many centuries in the making, in the year 1054, Pope Leo IX of the Roman Catholic Church and the patriarch of Constantinople, Michael Cerularius, officially split from each other into what is today the Western Church and the Eastern Church. The mutual excommunications imposed upon each other by both Church leaders way back then were finally ended in 1965.

• To the best of my recollection, as a Catholic growing up in the late 1950s and '60s, I learned absolutely nothing in my religious education classes about any of the other Christian faiths, especially of the Eastern traditions. My first memory of what I would later discover to be Greek and Russian Orthodox Christians, Egyptian and Ethiopian Coptic Christians, and Armenian, Assyrian, and Syriac Christians, was while watching segments of Pope John XXIII's funeral on a fuzzy black-and-white television screen in 1963. And what I remembered most of these mysterious holy men as they passed by in homage to the deceased pope were their really elaborate robes and fascinatingly mysterious hats. Even when I learned about the Great Schism between the Eastern and Western Churches in high school history classes, the theological meaning and context was completely lost on me.

• My purpose in sharing this childhood recollection is to suggest that one of the reasons we in the Western Churches (which include both the original united Roman Catholic traditions and the subsequent faiths that appeared after the Reformation) don't know very much about the lives of half of the Twelve Apostles is a result of the animosity that resulted in the Schism. Partly as the result of the outreaches started by Patriarch Athenagoras I and Pope Paul VI—and expanded upon hugely by John Paul II—we now have a chance to someday close the divide that has separated us for almost a millennium.

Before proceeding any further with the missionary journeys of the apostle Jude, I need to make two distinctions. The first—and easiest—is that from now on in this chapter, I will refer to him as Thaddaeus. I will do so because the vast majority of what the world knows about the apostle is intimately associated with the history of the Eastern Church. These Churches refer to him as Thaddaeus almost without exception.

The other involves a hugely controversial debate as to whether the apostle Thaddaeus (as one of the Twelve Apostles of Jesus) is the same person as the disciple Addai (one of the Seventy Disciples mentioned in Luke's Gospel) mentioned by Eusebius of Caesarea. This distinction between these two men is of no small consequence, especially as it pertains to recent research regarding, of all things, the famous holy relic, the Shroud of Turin. Even though scholars and theologians are all over the place on this issue, after many hours of wading through the ancient texts, my humble analysis is that yes, they are the same person.

The Missionary Journey of the Apostle Jude /Thaddaeus

According to the apocryphal Acts of the Holy Apostle Thaddaeus, One of the Twelve, Thaddaeus was born in the then Syrian city of Edessa, a city located along the Euphrates River in south central Turkey. Today, the city is known as Sanliurfa. He was a Hebrew born with the name Lebbaeus. As a young man he traveled to Jerusalem for a religious festival, a 600-mile journey over good Roman roads, and while in the region of the Jordan River valley, heard a desert preacher named John the Baptist speak. So impressed was the future apostle with the message of the prophet that he ultimately was baptized by John. And John, perhaps also impressed by this "man of heart," gave him the name Thaddaeus. And while traveling with the Baptist, he met Jesus.

After John the Baptist's execution by Herod, Thaddaeus then became a follower of Jesus, first as one of the Seventy Disciples and then as one of the Twelve Apostles. After the crucifixion of the Lord and day of Pentecost, very little is known with certainty of Thaddaeus's missionary journeys. Various Eastern Christian traditions have the apostle spreading the Gospel in the region of modern-day Lebanon, Syria, Turkey, and Iran. One consistent tradition has the apostle returning to his birth city of Edessa, possibly with — or at the bidding of — the apostle Thomas.

The ruler of Edessa at that time was a man named Abgar. Months prior to the crucifixion of Jesus, this king had some incurable disease, perhaps leprosy or consumption. Hearing of the miracles being performed by this Galilean preacher, Abgar dispatched a letter to Him asking if He would travel to his city to cure him. In return, he offered Jesus sanctuary from the "wicked plottings of the Jerusalem Sanhedrin."

According to the Armenian Church tradition, Jesus actually answered Abgar's request. The forth-century Church father Eusebius of Caesarea claimed to have actually read the

Image of the Shroud of Edessa
Courtesy of WikiCommons

letters, as did the Spanish pilgrim/nun, Egeria, in 384 AD. In His remarkable reply to the king's request, Jesus ultimately declined his offer. He, instead, sent this message: "Peace to thee and thy city! For because of this I am come, to suffer for the world, and to rise again, and to raise up the forefathers. And after I have been taken up into the heavens I shall send thee my disciple Thaddaeus, who shall enlighten thee, and guide thee into all the truth, both thee and thy city."

True to His word, immediately after Pentecost, Thaddaeus traveled to Edessa. As a result of his rock-solid faith in the earthly mission of Jesus Christ, Abgar was healed by the apostle of his affliction. In the tradition of the Armenian Church,

---

The Image of Edessa

The Image of Edessa (also known as the Mandylion) brought to King Apgar by the apostle Thaddaeus was thought to be the burial cloth of the Crucified Jesus. History says it only portrayed the Lord's face. Recently, there has been a book written by the author Ian Wilson in which he presents a very compelling case for the Image of Edessa actually being the Shroud of Turin folded into fours.

---

part of the miraculous recovery involved the Image of Edessa (also referred to as the Mandylion). In gratitude for this miraculous cure, Edessa became the first recorded city in history to accept Christianity. After baptizing many thousands of new converts and establishing many churches, Thaddaeus left Edessa forever.

Khor Virap Monastery, With Noah's Grapes and Mt. Ararat

Place of the Final Farwell Between the Apostles Thaddaeus and Bartholomew

Although there are conflicting traditions, it is generally thought that he next traveled north and westward through the region of eastern Turkey around Lake Van. He then continued northward to the region of modern-day Armenia (the ancient biblical land of the kingdom of Urartu) at the base of holy Mt. Ararat. Here the apostle would have celebrated the Eucharist with wine produced from vines originally cultivated by old Noah himself.

Portrait of Jude Thaddeaus and Bartholomew
Khor Virap Monastery

He also met up with one of his brother Twelve, the apostle Bartholomew, and

evangelized the surrounding region. The present-day Khor Virap Monastery is
located at the place where tradition says the two men of God reunited. From here, after one last final goodbye, Bartholomew continued his missionary journey west and south to Azerbaijan and southeast Turkey, and Thaddeaus headed eastward into ancient Persia.

And it would be there in around 60 AD, fifty miles from the summit of Mt. Ararat in what is today northwest Iran, that Jude Thaddaeus would meet his martyrdom. Both local tradition and Armenian Church history strongly support this location and date. It was just twelve years after Pentecost. In that year, in the town of Shavarshan in the Ardaz province, Thaddaeus baptized Santoukhd, the daughter of the local king. When the news of her conversion reached her father, he was furious. He then ordered all Christians killed — including his daughter and the apostle.

A church and monastery was built over the site of his original grave in around the year 66 in what is today the West Azerbaijan Province, Iran. This Church of St. Thaddaeus still stands. (As of this writing, because of its remoteness and of the difficult foreign relations my country has with Iran, this is one of the very few places I discuss in this book that I have not visited. I did get to within forty-five miles of the church during our ascent of Mt. Ararat.)

The Saint of Lost Causes

In the early years of the Christian Church, St. Jude/Thaddeaus was rarely venerated because people were afraid of their prayers being mistakenly sent to the other Judas, the apostle who betrayed the Lord in the Garden of Gethsemane. Over time, pilgrims who did pray for St. Jude's intercession very often found their prayer wishes granted. One theory for this success is that the apostle was so anxious to help anyone because of his ostracism that he went overboard in his intercessions. Years later, St. Bridget of Sweden and St. Bernard of Clairvaux had visions from God telling them to share with the world His wish for St. Jude to forever bear the title of "The Patron Saint of the Impossible."

However, a minor tradition that I found seems equally interesting. The time frame also fits closer to what Professor Plinio Corrêa de Oliveira said with regards to the apostle Simon: "In 1605, the relics of the two Apostles were transported to the Vatican Basilica and placed in a crypt under the Altar of the Crucifixion." The theory holds that even after the Muslim conquest of 750 AD, out of respect for the great man of God, the Caliphs allowed both the Church of St. Thaddaeus and the apostle's relics to remain undisturbed. It was in response to the thirteenth-century invasion of Armenia by the Mongols, with their scorched-earth policy of destroying everything they invaded, that Jude Thaddaeus's bones were finally removed from their rest.

St. Thaddaeus Monastery, West Azerbaijan Province, Iran
Courtesy of WikiCommons

Visiting Jude Thaddaeus's Remains Today

The vast majority of the apostle's earthly remains are in the crypt below the Altar of St. Joseph in the left transept of the Vatican. His bones are commingled with those of the apostle Simon. How and when the apostle arrived there seems to be a

The Church of St. Lazarus, Larnaca, Cypress

complete mystery. And just like the chapter on Simon, a very exhaustive search of history yielded only two possibilities. The first is the belief that since the two apostles are in eternal rest together, they were smuggled out of Mesopotamia together, probably as a response to the eighth-century Muslim conquest. Being as the site of the two apostles' original burials were only about 125 miles apart from each other, logically, this theory is possible.

A second theory is more compelling. Aristocrats and other affluent Armenian families who were able to do so, escaped the onslaught of the marauding hordes by fleeing to the island of Cypress off the west coast of Turkey. Here they would ultimately become mingled, both in bloodlines and commerce, with the royal families of Europe. The remains of the apostle were very likely brought to the island at this time to protect them from desecration.

There Jude Thaddaeus rested once again—possibly alongside the remains of his old acquaintance, Lazarus, in the crypt of St. Lazarus Basilica in the city of Larnaca, Cyprus. Here they stayed until the Ottoman conquest of the island in 1570.

Crypt of St. Lazarus Church with Two Empty Coffins

Visitors to the crypt to this very day can still see the two empty stone coffins sitting side by side. From there, the bones of the apostle traveled to Rome and St. Peter's Basilica, probably via Venice. As an aside, Lazarus's mortal remains ultimately traveled to Marseilles, France, via Constantinople.

St. James the Less Holding the Instrument of His
Martyrdom: A Fuller's Club

Chapter Six
The Apostle James the Less, Son of Alphaeus

> These are the twelve He appointed: Simon (to whom he gave the name Peter), James son of Zebedee and his brother John . . . Thomas, James son of Alphaeus, Thaddaeus, Simon the Zealot and Judas Iscariot, who betrayed him. Mark 3:16–19 NIV

The apostle James the Less is the most controversial figure of all of the Twelve Apostles. Uncountable page after page of uncountable treatises have been produced over the last two millennia trying to analyze and deduce just who this man actually was. A very minor tradition portrays him as an obscure apostle whose apostolic work we know almost nothing about. Or, as the majority of early Church Fathers and religious scholars right up until this day only bitterly agree, he was such an important figure in the first Jerusalem church that even the apostles Peter and Paul deferred to his authority!

He is mentioned with certainty only as James, the son of Alphaeus, in the Gospels of Mark, Luke, Matthew, and Acts when the evangelists all formally list the Twelve Apostles. John does not list him at all (nor for reasons unknown, does he mention the apostles Matthew and Simon the Zealot). What makes this apostle so controversial is, of course, the fact that the name James appears so often in the New Testament.

• James, the son of Zebedee and brother of John, referred to as "James the Greater." This James's place in the history of the Twelve is without controversy.
• James, the son of Alpheus, mentioned in the lists of the apostles Mark, Matthew, Luke, and Acts.
• James the Less mentioned in Mark 15:40, the son of Mary and

brother of Joseph and Salome.
- The brother of Jude in Jude 1:1 named James.
- And possibly the most contentious James of all, James, the brother of the Lord and bishop of the Church of Jerusalem.

Compounding this mystery of the identity of the apostle James the Less is just exactly what it was that the New Testament writers actually meant by the word "brother/ brethren" and how the word pertains to the doctrinal concept of the perpetual virginity of Mary, the mother of Jesus. Beginning with Irenaeus, the bishop of Lyon (130–202 AD), and then enlarged upon by Origen of Alexandria (185–254), the belief in Mary's perpetual virginity was later affirmed by several ecumenical councils. The belief is still part of the doctrines of the all Catholic, Eastern Orthodox, some Anglican Churches, and the Assyrian Churches of the East. Although Martin Luther supported the doctrine, many Reformed Protestant traditions have abandoned the belief.

For the sake of this book—and only after much, much study—I am going to side with the vast majority of theologians, saints, and scholars who have concluded that the identity of the Apostle James the Less, the son of Alpheus, and James, the brother of the Lord and first bishop of the Church of Jerusalem are all the same person. Here are some of my reasons:

- Galatians 1:18–19 NIV: "Then after three years, I [Paul] went up to Jerusalem to get acquainted with Cephas and stayed with him fifteen days. I saw none of the other apostles—only James, the Lord's brother."
- Papias, bishop of Hierapolis (70–163 AD), and a man who was actually taught by the apostle John, states that James, son of Alphaeus, is the same person as James the Less.
- A careful reading of St. Jerome's (347–420 AD) *The Perpetual Virginity of Blessed Mary*: In this lengthy tome, Jerome goes into great detail upon the Old and New Testaments' usage of the term "brother" and/or "brethren."

• And the simplest reason of all is that there is no valid competing tradition as to the life and martyrdom of James the Less, other than that he was the bishop of Jerusalem.

James the Less is the only member of the Twelve Apostles who never left Jerusalem after the death of Jesus. His mother stood by Mary, the mother of Jesus, at the base of His Cross. It is also very likely that he was the first of the Twelve to actually see and speak with the risen Jesus. St. Jerome and the early Church father, Epiphanius of Cyprus (310–403 AD), state that at His ascension, Jesus told the eleven apostles (minus, of course, Judas Iscariot) that he wanted James to guide His new church in Jerusalem. Until his martyrdom just over thirty years later, James would serve as the church's first bishop.

Before being personally chosen by Jesus to be one of His Twelve, Hegesippus (110–180 AD), a chronicler of the early Christian Church, described James as follows: "He was always a virgin, and was a Nazarite" [one who is consecrated from his birth to the Lord]. In consequence of which he was never shaved, never cut his hair, never drank any wine or other strong liquor; moreover he never used any bath, or oil to anoint his limbs, and never ate of any living creature except when of precept, as the paschal lamb: he never wore sandals, never used any other clothes than one single linen garment. He prostrated so much in prayer that the skin of his knees and forehead was hardened like to camels' hoofs."

James was martyred in Jerusalem during Passover in the year 62 AD. The apostle's death has been well described by Eusebius of Caesarea, St. Jerome, and the Jewish historian Josephus. In that year, a newly appointed high priest of the Jerusalem temple named Ananus decided to take drastic action in a futile attempt to stem the growth of the new Christian Church. Thinking he could take advantage of the huge crowd of worshipers visiting Jerusalem for the Passover feast, he had James brought up to the top of one of the Temple walls. Here the new priest felt he could intimidate the bishop of Jerusalem into denying that Jesus is the Messiah and the Son of God.

But rather than doing so, the apostle took advantage of the opportunity to praise and glorify the Lord; it was said that many hundreds of listeners were converted. Enraged by the

The Walled Temple Mount in the Old City of Jerusalem
Location of the Jewish Temple in the Days of the Apostle James.
Presently Occupied by the Dome of the Rock Mosque

audacity of James's disobedience, Ananus ordered him thrown from the wall. The apostle survived the fall, and even though both his legs were broken, he continued to preach the good news of Jesus. Wishing to silence him, the high priest ordered James stoned. When this did not work either, a member of the crowd stepped forward and beat him to death with a fuller's club. (Laundrymen in ancient times were called fullers, and they used clubs to help beat clean clothes.)

Visiting James the Less's Remains Today

James the Less was originally buried near the Jerusalem Temple where he was originally killed. The early Church Fathers speak of a small column that originally marked his grave. centuries later, about 100 years after Constantine declared Christianity the religion of the Roman Empire, the Armenian patriarch in Jerusalem built a small Byzantine church over the spot where the apostle James the Greater was beheaded by Herod Agrippa. This church was completed in 420 and shortly afterward, the remains of James the Less were moved into the new sanctuary as well.

Here the bones of the apostle James the Less rested for only one hundred years. At this time his mortal remains were translated to the Church of the Holy Apostles (Santi XII Apostoli) in Rome. This church was founded by Pope Pelagius I (556–561) and was completed by his successor, Pope John III (561–574). It was originally dedicated to the apostles Philip and James the Less. To visit the tomb of James the Less, all you have to do is circle to the left side of the church and descend the stairs in to the crypt. There, below the main altar, are the ossuary of both James and Philip.

Ossuary in the Crypt below the Main Altar of the Church of the Holy Apostles, Rome, Italy

The Apostle Philip Subduing the Hieropolis Dragon/Snake

Chapter Seven

29 y8⁵ ## The Apostle Philip

> The next day Jesus decided to leave for Galilee. Finding Philip, he said to him, "Follow me." John 1:43 NIV

Other than including him in their listings of the Twelve, the synoptic Gospels of Mark, Luke, and Matthew say nothing else about the apostle Philip. Only in John's Gospel do we have an opportunity to learn something of him. There is very little written by scholars and theologians of the reason(s) why this is so. One theory I found says that because Philip was not part of the group of four apostles who were closest to Jesus (Peter, John, James the Greater, and Andrew) that the writers of the synoptic Gospels chose simply to leave him out. Another theory says that because John and Philip's hometown, Bethsaida, was the same, that they were very likely childhood friends. Also, and probably more important, their final missionary territories of Ephesus and Hierapolis in Asia Minor (present-day Turkey) were only around 120 miles away from each other. This would have given them several years to interact after the Resurrection of Jesus, and his recollections of Philip would have been fresh in John's memory when he was writing his Gospel.

We learn in the Gospel of John that it was Jesus who actually sought out Philip to be one of His followers with the authoritative call: "Follow Me." Philip, in turn, would bring Bartholomew to Jesus. Because Philip is a Greek name (meaning lover of horses), scholars are confident that he was probably a Greek-educated, Hellenized Jew. It is thought that he was of upper-class status and had some authority outside of his being among Jesus's Twelve. This is because in John 12:20–22, Philip is asked by a group of Gentile Greeks for an introduction to Jesus.

We know that at least twice, Philip demonstrated that even though he walked with Jesus during nearly His entire three-year earthly ministry, he didn't quite grasp completely the full meaning of the Lord's mission. At the Feeding of the Five

Thousand, when asked by Jesus how they would obtain enough food to feed the multitudes, the apostle essentially said that he had no idea what to do. Later on in John's Gospel, while dining with the Lord at the Last Supper — the supreme moment when you'd think that the entirety of the Twelve would have had His mission all figured out — Philip, in one final moment of human weakness and doubt, innocently asks of Jesus, "Lord, show us the Father, and that will be enough for us." The apostle was instantly and summarily admonished by a frightened and frustrated Jesus: "Don't you know me, Philip, even after I have been among you such a long time? Anyone who has seen me has seen the Father. How can you say, 'Show us the Father'? Don't you believe that I am in the Father, and that the Father is in me?" John 14:9–10 NIV.

Like the rest of the Twelve, Philip was with Jesus to witness to the miracle of the wedding at Cana, to the Lord's encounter with the Samaritan woman at the well, to Jesus's ascension into heaven. In the book of Acts, along with the rest of his fellow apostles, he laid his hands upon and blessed the seven deacons, who included the soon-to-be martyred Steven, as well as his namesake, the evangelist Philip. One potentially very sad moment in his time with Jesus and His earthly ministry was to sit by silently (along with his fellow Bethsaida home boys, Andrew, Peter, John, and James) while a rarely seen angry Lord cursed his hometown.

From Matthew 11:20–24 NIV: "Then Jesus began to denounce the towns in which most of his miracles had been performed, because they did not repent. "Woe to you, Chorazin! Woe to you, Bethsaida! For if the miracles that were performed in you had been performed in Tyre and Sidon, they would have repented long ago in sackcloth and ashes. But I tell you, it will be more bearable for Tyre and Sidon on the Day of Judgment than for you. And you, Capernaum, will you be lifted to the heavens? No, you will go down to Hades. For if the miracles that were performed in you had been performed in Sodom, it would have remained to this day. But I tell you that it will be more bearable for Sodom on the Day of Judgment than for you."

Before continuing with the missionary journeys of Philip, it is important at this critical point to remember not to confuse the apostle with Philip the evangelist (Acts 21:8), even though they both displayed an instinct for evangelism. They did know each other, however; Philip, as one of the apostles, prayed for and laid hands on Philip the evangelist (Acts 6:6) at the beginning of the latter's deaconship. Even though they journeyed to nearly opposite regions of the known world, the two are very often conflated in various religious traditions and scholarly research.

Like the rest of Jesus's Twelve Apostles, although he may have seemed confused and uncertain of His message during His earthly life, after Pentecost, Philip would indeed redeem himself and become a true workhorse in the service of the Lord. After Pentecost and the dispersion of the Twelve, there is a strong tradition of the apostle Philip going at first to preach to the Gauls in the region that is today southern France.

My research seems to suggest that Philip is the only member of the Twelve who has any tradition at all in France. He preached for several years the good news of Jesus Christ around the area of the modern-day city of Marseille, assisted for awhile by Joseph of Arimathea. Arriving there from ancient Judea would not have been any great hardship for Philip. Sea routes discovered by the ancient Phoenicians a thousand years before, originally for the trading of tin from the British Isles, were well traveled and reliable. Joseph, of course, as a result of his involvement in the tin trade, would have been well-known to the Jews of the region.

Joseph of Arimathea, as I mentioned earlier, would continue after a time northward to the British Isles, where he would set up the island's first Christian church in Glastonbury. An interesting historical note is that shortly after the death of Steven and the ensuing persecutions, the three Marys who were witness to the death and Resurrection of Jesus—Mary Magdalene, Mary the mother of James and John, and Mary, wife of Cleopas — all traveled as well to Gaul. They originally landed at a spot near the modern-day city of Marseille called Les Saintes Maries de la Mer (The Holy Marys from the Sea).

After preaching to the Gauls in southern France, there is very little reliable information as to Philip's travels until he arrived at Hieropolis, the city in Turkey where he would be ultimately martyred. The forth-century apocryphal book, The Acts of Philip, has the apostle stopping in Athens, Greece, for two years. Here, he baptized over 500 citizens, founded a church, and installed a bishop. He then departed for the ancient Asian kingdoms of Phrygia and Lydia, which is roughly in the region of modern-day central Turkey. While there, he crossed paths with the apostles Peter and John. Tradition says that Philip asked Peter, "I pray you strengthen me, that I may go and preach like you." It was in this region that he joined with Bartholomew for a while. After a short period of time, the two of them, accompanied by Philip's daughters, traveled to the ancient city of Hieropolis.

Tourist Map of the Ancient Roman City of Heiropolis, Parmukkale,Turkey

Church tradition and biblical scholarship pretty much

agree with the fact that the apostle Philip eventually settled in the former Greco/Roman city of Hieropolis. Now a UNESCO World Heritage site, the ruins of the city sit on a hilltop above the modern Turkish city of Pamukkale. The earliest documentation of the apostle Philip's missionary work, martyrdom, and burial were in a letter written in 190 AD by the Church Father, Polycrates of Ephesus (130–196) to the bishop of Rome. A portion of the letter is quoted by the Church historian, Eusebius of Caesarea: "For in Asia, also, great luminaries have fallen asleep, who shall rise again on the last day during the *parousia* [Greek word meaning arrival] of the Lord when He comes with glory out of heaven to gather all the saints, [including] Philip, of the twelve apostles, who sleeps in Hierapolis and his two daughters ..."

When Philip and Bartholomew first arrived in Hierapolis, they discovered the city had a strong snake-worshiping cult. One of Philip's first acts was to do battle with a giant snake (some legends say it was a dragon) and ultimately destroy it. This act, along with his passionate and inspired preaching, led a majority of the citizens of the region to convert to Christianity. Around the year 62 AD, the apostle performed a healing miracle upon the wife of the Roman proconsul Nicanora, which led to her conversion to Christianity.

This so enraged her husband that he ordered Philip's death (as well as Bartholomew's and Philip's sister Mariamne) by crucifixion. Legend says that Philip preached from the cross until his final breath. He was then buried in a nearby grave. As an aside, the legend also says that there was something so convincing in his sermons that the local governor had Bartholomew and Mariamne released from their cross in order to continue his mission.

My Visit to Hieropolis

About a three-hour drive east of the Mediterranean town of Ephesus is the ancient city of Hieropolis. Greek for "Holy

City," her ruins today sit upon a flattened hilltop just north of the modern-day Turkish city of Pamukkale. Since her founding in the second-century BC – and continuing to this very day – the

city, with her thermal springs, mineral baths, and dazzling white travertine cliffs, has served as a healing center and spa as well as a tourist attraction. I recall wondering out loud as we sat next to one of the hot spring pools how, in this very conservative Muslim country, all of the teenage Russian and Eastern European tourists were allowed to get away with wearing the skimpiest of bikinis!

Martyrium of St. Philip, Looking North. The Main Altar is in the Center

At the highest point of this now World Heritage site, are the ruins of the Martyrium (memorial church) of St. Philip. The

High Altar, Church of St. Philip, Pamukkale, Turkey

Original Burial Site of the Apostle Philip, Pamukkale, Turkey

high altar of this formerly huge eight-sided basilica is located over the crucifixion site of the apostle Philip. Visitors today can still walk up the long trail from the city center that pilgrims have walked since the third century. Just recently discovered (rediscovered?) right next to the ruins of the former church are several tombs, one of which was the original tomb of Philip. The tomb, as was expected by the Italian archaeologist doing the excavation, did not contain the relics of the apostle.

This is because the final resting place of the apostle Philip is in the Basilica Santi Apostoli (Church of the Holy Apostles) in Rome, right beside the mortal remains of his fellow apostle, James the Less. Philip's body was very probably first removed from its Hieropolis tomb by the emperor Constantine (or his son, Constantius the second) who had it translated to his new Church of the Holy Apostles in Constantinople. His remains were then acquired by Pope John the Third (560–572 AD) and were brought to Rome, where they have rested since in the Church of the Holy Apostles Philip and James the Less.

The Apostle James the Greater, With His Scallop Shell,
Pilgrim's Hat, and Staff

Chapter Eight
The Apostle James the Greater, Son of Zebedee

> It was about this time that King Herod arrested some who belonged to the church, intending to persecute them. He had James, the brother of John, put to death with the sword. Acts 12:1–2 NIV

With this simple declarative sentence from the book of the Acts of the Apostles, James, the son of Zebedee and the brother of John, becomes the only member of the Twelve Apostles of Jesus whose cause of death can known with absolute certainty by New Testament readers. Not counting, of course, the former apostle, Judas Iscariot. But before discussing this first of the Twelve to suffer martyrdom, as a bit of a change in format, I'd like to share a story. I first read this story in a book titled *Virgin Trails: A Secular Pilgrimage*, by Robert Ward. My paraphrasing from the chapter titled, "Our Lady of the Boat," does Mr. Ward's original telling of this beautiful story only partially adequate justice.

At the farthest western point of Spain's Camino de Santiago (Way of St. James) there is a very interesting—and somewhat poignant—tradition associated with the apostle's conscious decision to undergo martyrdom. On a boulder-strewn beach just west of the Spanish village of Muxia, overlooking the vastness that is the Atlantic Ocean, stands the small church of Our Lady of the Boat. The chapel was built to honor both the mother of Jesus and the historic decision made by the apostle James as he sat upon one of these huge rocks. Allotted by the Lord to spread the Good News to the souls of the Iberian Peninsula, he had at last reached this awe-inspiring "end of the land."

The good apostle was physically tired, emotionally beaten down, and was suffering from just a bit of self-pity. The seemingly impossible task of trying to get the pagan Celtic people who inhabited this region of the world to which he had been assigned to give up their ancient beliefs and to hear the words of Jesus had finally overwhelmed him. He was having serious doubts about the effectiveness of his Gospel mission. In his mind he saw himself as a failure. Church history would prove otherwise! Likewise, James was homesick. He longed with all his heart to be back in Israel, back to his childhood home along the Sea of Galilee, and back with his friends and fellow apostles in Jerusalem.

Church of Our Lady of the Boat, Muxia, Spain

As he sat there on that beach on what was probably a gorgeous sunny day, he began to see far off in the distance a small boat approaching. As the vessel drew nearer, he saw that standing in its prow was a woman, a woman he knew very well. The woman was Mary, the mother of his beloved friend Jesus! James attempted to get up to meet her, but before he could rise, she was standing beside him. After comforting the tired apostle by first assuring him that he was, indeed, having great success, the Holy Mother laid her hand on his head and offered him two alternatives. "James, my precious Son says that you have been a faithful and hardworking servant, and that He and those you have touched with His words will be eternally grateful. But he feels your pain, and He wants to give you a choice: Either you stay here in Spain and continue your work among these lost souls or return to Jerusalem, where much work also needs to be done."

Mary then lifted her hand from the apostle, stepped back, and with a look of infinite compassion—and perhaps just a touch of sadness—continued speaking. "My Son says that if you choose to return home, your works there are much needed and will be appreciated as well; however, a violent death awaits you. You, most dear James, will have the distinction of being the first of your brother Twelve Apostles to be martyred in His name." And with that, the blessed mother was gone. Immediately the apostle began his long journey back to Jerusalem.

The books of Matthew, Luke, Mark, and Acts list the apostle James as simply James or James, the son of Zebedee. John's Gospel lists him as one of the sons of Zebedee. The apostle historically has been referred to as James "the Greater" or the James "the Major." These various designations assigned to him by theologians and biblical scholars down through the years are thought to simply prevent confusion with the other apostle James, son of Alphaeus. The exact reason for this greater/lesser designation, however, is lost in the mists of time and is still a hot topic of debate, with no obvious theory providing a firm answer. It's possible James the Greater was physically a large man or his inner-circle relationship with Jesus may have given the apostle more prestige.

James and his brother John were the sons of a fisherman named Zebedee, and they lived until James's young adulthood near the town of Bethsaida on the north shore of the Sea of Galilee. The Gospel of Matthew 4:21–22 NIV has Jesus calling to him and his brother as they were with their father repairing their nets. It is very likely that his brother John, a follower of John the Baptist, had already instilled the essence of Jesus's earthly mission in James long before their calling. Salome, one of the women who were with Jesus at His crucifixion and who helped to anoint His body after His death, is traditionally thought to be James's and John's mother.

James is mentioned several times in the New Testament. The evangelist Mark, in his listing of the Twelve, adds the nickname *Boanerges* to the names of James and his brother, which tradition says means "Sons of Thunder." Again, there are a lot of theories as to why, but it is most likely that one or both of them was loud, boisterous, and impetuous. Theologians point to an episode in Luke 9:51–56, where the brothers asked Jesus if they could "command fire to come down from heaven" to punish a Samaritan village that refused them hospitality as one example of their impatience. Another would be where James and John (or their mother) had the audacity to ask Jesus to grant them seats on His right and left when He achieved His glory.

James did, however, seem to have (along with Peter and John) some sort of a special relationship with Jesus. The three apostles are recorded in the New Testament as being the only witnesses to Jesus's transfiguration. In Luke 8:49–56, where Jesus raises Jarius's daughter back to life, Jesus specifically asks to exclude everyone from entering the house except James, Peter, and John. Lastly, the three men were the only apostles mentioned in the Gospels who were with Jesus (and infamously fell asleep) during His agony in the Garden of Gethsemane.

This special relationship between James, Peter, and John, however, is notably missing in the New Testament after Pentecost. This supports the stories that James immediately afterwards had departed Jerusalem to begin his missionary journeys. With the ancient Church having not yet fallen under the influence of Paul's inclusion of the Gentiles, James set out on his commission following Jesus's original proclamation to "Preach to the lost sheep of the house of Israel." Traveling along the very well established trade routes westward across the Mediterranean Sea, the apostle's first stop would be the island of Sardinia.

The early Jewish historian Josephus spoke in his writings of how in the year 19 AD, there were 4,000 Jewish youths from Palestine who were captured and conscripted into the Roman army and sent to Sardinia. These men were believed to have been followers of Judas of Galilee, an early Messianic prophet mentioned in the book of Acts. Some may even have known of the works of John the Baptist. It was among these Jewish soldiers and slaves that James first preached the Gospel.

Church tradition says that James's missionary journey next took him to the Iberian Peninsula, home the modern-day countries of Spain and Portugal. Using the most likely date of 30 AD as the date of the first Christian Pentecost, it would be only fourteen years between the beginning of James's travels and his martyrdom. Of course, he didn't know it when he set out from Jerusalem on that springtime of the year that he was going to be the first of the Twelve to be martyred and that his time to accomplish this seemingly impossible missionary journey would be cut so short. It is because of this short time span that a minority of scholars say that James, the son of Zebedee, never really made it to Spain. Their faulty deduction behind their theories is that this was just too great an area for anyone to accomplish so much in so little time.

They're wrong for three big reasons. The first is that there is a long-standing, irrefutable local tradition everywhere you go on the Iberian Peninsula that the apostle James brought Christianity to this area of the world. It is easy to be dismissive of the nonscientific concept of "local tradition," but we are not dealing with objective science with regards to the apostles. We are talking about twelve men who walked the earth with the Son of God, who were endowed by the Holy Spirit at Pentecost, and whose selfless and unconditional dedication to the Word of God would lead all but one of them to a violent death. Because nobody can know with absolute certainty the exact answer, all we have in James's case (and with many of the other members of the Twelve) is local tradition. I note at this time as well, an equally important second part of my firm faith in local tradition—at least as it regards James: There is no other place on the planet that makes any claims to having been evangelized by him.

A second advantage that James had was that this area of the ancient western Mediterranean was not some primitive backwater or unexplored terra incognito as many may think. Ancient Roman-era seafaring maps show quite clearly that there were well-established trade routes linking all of the great port cities of the Mediterranean, as well as extending beyond the Straits of Gibraltar all the way up to the British Isles. Even a millennia before the Romans arrived on the scene, these seagoing highways were used by the Greeks, the Carthaginians, and, stretching as far back as 1200 BC, by the Phoenicians. Using modern-day mapping programs, the apostle's springtime land and sea voyage from Jerusalem to the northern Sardinia city of Olbia would take, on the average, twenty-five days.

Iberia's Roman System of Roads in 30 AD
Courtesy of Wikipedia

Another part of this traveling equation was the predominance throughout all of the Roman Empire of the great Roman roads. The superhighways of their day, these ancient engineering marvels are what made living and traveling in that period of history as effortless as was then humanly possible. So well were these roads constructed that many still exist into our time, over 2,000 years later. By the time the apostle James arrived in Spain, probably at the southeast coastal port city of Gedes (modern-day Cadiz), the Romans had been on the Iberian Peninsula for over 200 years.

This relatively safe and secure system of roads would give him quick access to the rest of the region.

The final concept to keep in mind with regards to James's mission was, again, that he had left Jerusalem just after Pentecost with the sole mission of spreading the good news of Jesus to the "lost sheep of the house of Israel." That is, the Jewish people dispersed throughout the known world at the time. This holy mandate to concentrate on the Jews of Spain and not have to be overly concerned with the vast majority of the country's Gentiles would save the apostle a lot of work.

Many readers may be surprised to discover that there were very significant numbers of Jews on the Iberian Peninsula at the time of the apostle's arrival. One of the greatest evidences for such is that many historians associate the modern-day region of northwestern Spain with that of the ancient land of Tarshish of Old Testament fame.

To help in his building of the first Jewish temple, 1 Kings 10:22 says that King Solomon allied himself with King Hiram of Tyre, who had "the fleet of ships of Tarshish that once every three years would arrive bringing gold, silver, ivory, apes, and peacocks." As well, the king most likely would have sent along Jewish emissaries, traders, and laborers to help in this endeavor. Also, over the following centuries, rabbinic commentators speak of Jews settling upon the Iberian Peninsula following the destruction of the First Temple by the Babylonian king Nebuchadnezzar as well as the multitude of expulsions of Jews from the Holy Lands by various Roman emperors.

The locations of James's exact travels while on his mission to Spain are not possible to know with any certainty. The only traditions we have that place him on the Iberian Peninsula while still alive are the legends of his visions of the Virgin Mary in January AD 40 in the Roman city of Caesaraugusta (modern-day Zaragoa) and the episode of his call to martyrdom by the mother of Jesus at Muxia in 43 AD that I shared at the beginning of this chapter. Even his mandate to preach to the lost tribes of Israel is complicated by the fact that during the expulsion of the Jewish people in 1492 by King Ferdinand and Queen Isabella, all records of their existence were destroyed.

But with the help of modern-day Internet searches, as well as various computer programs that are able to calculate time and distances of travel in the ancient Roman Empire, I believe that re-creating a very likely scenario of the apostle's travels is possible. The first thing that needed to be done was to map the cities on the Iberian Peninsula that had a Jewish population at the beginning of the first century. After doing this and then noting their locations on a map, I was left with what seemed like a random, absolutely unrelated hodgepodge of towns and communities. That was, however, until I laid a grid of Roman roads and navigatable rivers over them. The whole of ancient Spain then made nearly perfect sense.

The only choice that I needed to make now was where it was that James made landfall on the Iberian Peninsula. Logic would assume that before he departed from Jerusalem on his journey, the apostle would have consulted with people who would have some knowledge of his assigned missionary territories. And the most likely person with whom he would have spoken was the previously mentioned Joseph of Arimathea. The first of two cities that the two men may have considered as James's landfall in Hispania (the Roman word for Spain) after he would finish his mission on the island of Sardinia were the cities of Tarraco and Gedes.

In keeping with James's injunction to preach to the "lost sheep of Israel," and after calculating the time needed to visit as many of the Jewish communities in southern Spain as possible, the most logical place for him to have made landfall upon the Iberian Peninsula would have been the port city of Gedes (modern-day Cadiz) on the country's Atlantic coast. If done in the months of June or July, the voyage to this well established seaport would have been a twelve-day nonstop trip from the southern Sardinian city of Caralis.

The city was the richest of the port cities on the

southwestern coast of Spain. It is considered by many historians as the actual location of the biblical land of Tarshish; therefore, it would also be home to a large and very ancient Jewish community. Linguists even go so far as to note that the names Gedes/Cadiz may actually derive from the Hebrew word *Gadir*, which means city of Gad!

Regardless of this distinction, since the days of ancient Phoenicia, Gedes was a busy provisioning port and a major stopover for ships sailing farther northward to the silver mines in Spanish Galicia and the tin mines of the British Isles, and would have been well-known to Joseph of Arimathea. But most important of all was the city's location on the western terminus of the famous Roman road, the Via Augusta (also known as the Via Hercluea). This over-900-mile-long "superhighway" stretched from the seaport of Gedes/Cádiz on Spain's Atlantic coast to ultimately reach —after crossing over the Pyrenees

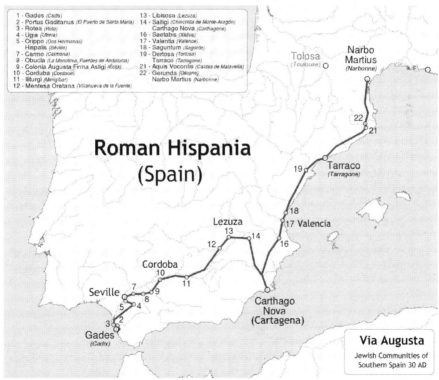

Map Courtesy of Wikipedia

Mountains — the Mediterranean Sea at Narvonne, France.

After James was finished setting up a Christian community in Gedes, he could travel northeastward either on the Via Augusta to the city of Seville or sail up the Guadalquivir River, which in Roman times was navigable all the way to the city of Cordoba. From there, the apostle could swing across central Spain's arid region of La Mancha to the city of Lezuza, following the road from there as it turned sharply southward to the Mediterranean port city of Carthago Nova, the modern-day city of Cartagena. Back on a seacoast again, James could have continued along the highway northward to Tarraco, the "City of the Jews." Or the former fisherman could have sailed up the coast, stopping at the Port of Valencia to spread the good news of Jesus.

In Tarraco (modern-day Tarragona), James would have found his largest Jewish audience. The long-established port city was captured from the native Iberian tribes by the Roman general, Gnaeus Cornelius Scipio, in 218 BC and served as a launching point for the rest of the conquest of Spain. Besides being of enormous strategic military importance, the region's

---

Saints Paul and Thecla

● Among the first-century New Testament apocrypha there is a document called the Acts of Paul and Thecla. It is an account of how St. Paul, on his first missionary journey, converted to Christianity a young virgin woman named Thecla while preaching in the city of Iconium (modern-day Konya, Turkey). After miraculously surviving burning at the stake and being thrown in an arena with wild animals, Thecla joined Paul in his quest to spread the Gospel.

● The book, however, never made it into the present-day New Testament canon. Beginning with the ancient Church Father, Tertullian, one theory for this omission was that the document seemed to legitimize a woman's right to both preach the word of God and to baptize.

● A local legend around the southeastern Spanish city of Tarraco says that in 50 AD (ten years after first being evangelized by the apostle James) that the St. Paul and his disciple Thecla established a church in Tarraco. St. Thecla is still the patron saint of the modern-day city of Tarragona.

fertile plains produced numerous agricultural commodities including flax. Tarraco's wines were prized throughout the entire Mediterranean Basin as the finest available. Historians date the Jewish settlement of this region to this early Roman period.

Once his work was started in Tarraco, the apostle James would then have had easy access to the heart of the Iberian Peninsula by the Roman road, Via Tarraconensis, or by sailing up the Ebro River. Either method of travel would have taken him to the city of Caesaraugusta, modern-day Zaragoza. Located on a bank of the Ebro River, it was in this city that religious scholars have some definitive evidence of the apostle James's presence in Spain.

The Apparition of the Virgin of El Pilar to St. James by Nicolas Enriquez
Courtesy of Wikicommons

During the first of two recorded apparitions recorded by the apostle, it is said that in January 40 AD, while he was praying along the banks of the river, the Virgin Mary appeared to him upon a column of jasper. The holy mother reassured James that his work in Spain was not in vain but at the time did not offer him a choice to quit as she would a few years later in Muxia. Afterward, she requested he build a church on the spot in her honor, which the obedient apostle then did. Today, the Basilica de Nuestra Senora del Pilar stands upon the very location of his vision. The church is believed to be the first church dedicated to the Virgin Mary in the world.

From Zaragoza, the apostle could continue his missionary journey northwestward up the Ebro River, visiting the isolated Jewish communities throughout the ancient kingdom of Aragon. After preaching the good news to the Roman city of Calahorra, the apostle could move westward on the Roman roads, through the present-day regions of the Basque Country, Navarre, Castile, and Asterias to the Roman military outposts of Pompleo (Pamplona), Legio VI Victrix (Leon,) and Asturica Augusta (Astorga.)

James was then in the region of western Spain known today as Galicia. The year was probably 42 or 43 AD. As stated in the legend of the church of Nosa Señora da Barca (Our Lady of the Boat), the good apostle was tired, despondent, and had literally stood at the edge of the known world; all this dedicated servant of the Lord wanted to do was go back home to Jerusalem. He journeyed from Asturica Augusta to what is today the region of the Atlantic coastal town of Muxia (the actual town did not exist until the fifth century) where, of course, he would receive his second vision of the Virgin Mary. This time she told the apostle that he could do whatever he wanted to do.

Cape Finisterre, Spain

Without a second of hesitation and anxious to start his journey home, he traveled the sixty miles northward to the seaport city of Brigantium (modern-day A Coruna). Used by the Phoenicians at least one thousand years before the time of James's life to provide silver and gold for King Solomon's First Temple—and very likely the first home of the Jewish people upon the Iberian Peninsula—this port city would soon play a part in the apostle's life once again.

But before returning to James's life back in Jerusalem, I'd like to take the liberty to reflect on his travels, especially upon Spanish Galicia. As he stood upon that rocky and harsh Atlantic beach and had his vision of the Holy Mother, he stood in the same area Christopher Columbus would stand fourteen centuries later, dreaming of a passage to Asia. The rugged and unforgiving coastal region would also give birth to the explorer Vasco da Gama, who would discover the sea route around the tip of Africa to the subcontinent of India.

As we'll learn in the chapter on Thomas, it would be in India that da Gama would encounter the millions of Christians who traced their apostolic authority back to this apostle. I wonder, as well, if the devoted apostle had any idea when he was traveling his last living journey in Spain, from Muxia to the port city of A Coruna, that as he passed through a low-lying area of countryside then called Composita Tella, that this site, which was no more than a Roman cemetery at the time, would end up being so very important to the world of Christianity.

In the apostle's day, the Roman road he traveled westward during his journey from the French Pyrenees across northern Spain, the Via Asturica Burdigalam, began in the modern-day Bordeaux region of France. It crossed the Pyrenees Mountains at the Roncesvalles Pass and terminated at the peninsula's western city of Asturica. This route follows almost exactly the modern-day Camino de Santiago, the Way of St. James, the same route millions of pilgrims would follow in the subsequent centuries to visit his grave in Santiago.

Finally, as James so passionately lamented to the Virgin Mary, Galicia would, indeed, prove to be the toughest and last region of the Iberian Peninsula to accept Christianity. The Celtic religious traditions were much ensconced in the region. However, once Galicia finally yielded, she would find herself guardian and keeper of our faithful servant's precious earthly remains.

James's Martyrdom

James returned to Jerusalem from his missionary journey to Spain in the year 43 or 44 AD. His sea and land voyage from the northwest Spanish port of Brigantium to Jerusalem, if taken during the summer months, would have taken the apostle around forty days. One can only imagine his profound joy upon his return home of seeing his mother and, very likely, his brother—and fellow apostle—John. Also, several others of the Twelve, including his dear friend Peter, would still be in Jerusalem as well. This would also be the first time he would meet Paul and hear of his work among the Gentiles. One great sadness of his returning home, was tht he missed the death of the Virgin Mary. He was hoping, I'm sure, to thank her for her encouraging words.

There are a couple of theories as to why James, son of Zebedee, was singled out for execution by the then king of Judea, Herod Agrippa. The first is that by the time of the arrival of James, Christians in Jerusalem had already become a severe annoyance to the Orthodox Jewish leaders and community. The Jewish historian, Josephus, wrote that Herod Agrippa was a pious and faithful Jew who wanted—at all costs—to repair the severely strained relationships with the Roman government. And James, a seasoned preacher, living up to his reputation of one of the "Sons of Thunder," was just creating too much conflict. Herod likely viewed the apostle as a devoted Christian who needed to be made an example.

Secondly, James may have been more successful than he may have thought in his evangelism of the Iberian Peninsula. His message of salvation may have stirred the hearts and minds of his followers to such a point that the apostle ended up an enemy of the state. Or it could have been a combination of both theories. That is, he arrived in Jerusalem in 43 or 44 AD an already marked man, and Agrippa, having had both a motive and a convenient solution, saw the execution of James as an opportunity to both do his patriotic duty to Rome and pacify the local authorities. As his grandfather, Herod the Great, had almost exactly forty-four years before with the crucifixion of a Galilean rabbi named Jesus, the king took advantage of the usual chaos that surrounded the Passover holiday in 44 AD to slay yet another Christian.

Visiting the Earthly Remains of the Apostle James, Son of Zebedee

In the Armenian Quarter of the old city of Jerusalem is the Armenian Apostolic Cathedral of St. James. This great church was built over the site of the beheading of James the Greater and is also the site of the former tomb of St. James the Less. A small chapel located near one of the main pillars of the cathedral contains an altar built over the apostle's skull.

To visit the rest of the earthly remains of St. James, a pilgrim must travel to the modern-day city of Santiago Compostela, in northwest Spain. Just how the great apostle's bones traveled from Jerusalem back to this distant Galician province he had just left a few years before is—like everything else in his life—a matter of some controversy. Many have the body of James miraculously (or not) arriving at the Atlantic seaport city of Iria Flavia (modern-day Padron), where it would then be forgotten during the invasion of the barbarians.

I don't completely rule out the miraculous nature of the journey; as noted before, these men were anointed with the power of the Holy Spirit and it is conceivable that anything could have happened. But it's just as plausible that the trip could have been made intentionally by some of his recent converts who were likely natives of Galicia. Perhaps, in spite of his protestations to the contrary as he was having his vision of the Holy Mother at Muxia, he actually did have a great fondness for the region, and his followers were just fulfilling his wishes to someday return there for good. There is also a second part to this final trip of his mortal remains to Galicia that no one, I believe, has ever considered.

Very shortly after the death of James the Greater, the persecutions taking place in the Holy Land continued to make life more and more unbearable for those of Jesus's inner circle of disciples and relatives. There is a strong tradition in southern France that around the year 45 AD, several of them, including Mary Magdalene; Mary, the mother of James the Less; and Mary Salome, the mother of John and James, either willingly left Jerusalem or, as some legends state, were set adrift in the Mediterranean by the Roman authorities. They ultimately landed in a small fishing village on the coast of Roman Gaul (southern France) that today is called Saintes Maries de la Mer.

One possibility is that Mary, the wife of Zebedee and mother of James and John, actually brought with her (either for safekeeping or to help fulfill James's wish to return to the Iberian Peninsula) the bones of her beloved son. Such a dangerous voyage at first may seem quite daunting. Although she was probably in her late sixties, she was an amazingly brave and strong-minded woman: recall that she had the fortitude and nerve to intercede on her sons' behalf to confront Jesus face-to-face regarding their sitting on either side of Him on His heavenly throne; she — and the other Marys — had the courage to remain at the foot of the Cross when nearly all others in the Lord's inner circle had run; and she had the courage to look into the empty tomb on that first Easter Sunday. With her other son, John, entrusted by Jesus Himself with the task of caring for His mother Mary, all Mary Salome had left in the world was James.

Why she didn't travel the rest of the way on the continuing sea voyage to Galicia will never be known. Perhaps the apostle had told her before he was martyred that he just wanted to be alone. The most likely reason was that she was old, and although from the nearby port of Marseille the journey to northwestern Spain would only take forty to fifty days, she was probably just plain worn out. She had lovingly sacrificed her sons and herself to Jesus, and now it was time for her to join Him in His heavenly kingdom. But we can only imagine her final sorrow when she handed the box containing her son's earthly remains over to his followers and said goodbye to him for the last time. A church was built over her grave in Saintes Maries de la Mer, and her tomb — along with Mary, mother of James the Less — can be visited to this day.

Cathedral of St. James, Santiago, Spain

The apostle's bones — minus his skull — arrived in Galicia probably at or near the Atlantic seaport city of Iria Flavia (modern-day Padron). With the help of local fishermen, his followers carried him inland to a location known only as *Contra Mare Britannicum* (Near the British Sea). Here, they took advantage of a well-established Roman cemetery located at an obscure place known only as *Composita Tella* (burial ground). There, as the result of the persecutions of Spanish Christians by Rome, the subsequent fall of the Roman Empire, and the invasion of Germanic tribes and then the Moors, the memory of the grave of James, the son of Zebedee, was forgotten for the next 800 years.

Although the exact location of the tomb may have been forgotten, a collective memory of the apostle being located in the region must have remained, because during those lost centuries, the area was home to Christian monks and hermits. And it was in the year 813 AD that one of these hermits named Palagio saw a dazzling light in the sky over what would turn out to be James's tomb. Under the guidance of a local bishop, Theodomirus, the cave/tomb was opened, and they found a sarcophagus with a placard that said: "Here lies Santiago, son of Zebedee and Salome, brother of St. John." The bishop then notified King Alfonso II of Asturias. The king granted an area of land three miles in all directions and ordered a shrine to James built over the grave. Several churches were subsequently built over the tomb, with the present-day cathedral completed in 1211.

Sarcophagus Containing the Relics of St. James, Son of Zebedee

To visit the bones of James, a pilgrim must travel to the Cathedral of St. James in the modern-day city of Santiago. Once inside this magnificent church, all a pilgrim has to do is climb down the stairs into the chamber beneath the main altar. You can then kneel down and look into the crypt where his remains rest in a gold and silver sarcophagus.

A grand tradition has arisen surrounding the remains of the apostle James, son of Zebedee and Salome. It is called the Camino de Santiago, the Way of St. James. For over a thousand years, millions of anonymous pilgrims, pious penitents, would-be adventurers, and just plain tourists have made their way to Santiago by foot, donkeys, bicycles, and automobiles for the sole purpose of visiting the city's famous cathedral and its precious holy relics. In medieval times, the Camino was considered one of the three mandatory pilgrimages

The Way of St. James

that every Christian, if able, had to participate in. The other two were a journey to Rome and to Jerusalem.

King Alfonso II's journey along the old Roman road, the Camino Privitivo, from his royal court in Oviedo to the tomb of Saint James is considered by Church historians as the first recorded pilgrimage. King Ferdinand and Queen Isabella of Spain were long ago themselves pilgrims on the Way of Saint

The Way of St. James

James, as were El Cid, Saint Francis of Assisi, King Louis VII of France, Dante, and most recently, the beloved Pope John Paul II.

Technically, the 1,000-year-old pilgrim trail known as El Camino de Santiago (the Way of Saint James) has no real beginning; you can start the journey from anywhere in the world. It does, however, have a clear and definitive end point: the northwestern Spanish city of Santiago de Compostela. The most popular of the Camino trails is the one that travels across the north of Spain called the French Route. Beginning high up in the Pyrenees Mountains in the village of Roncesvalles, the route snakes its way for more than six hundred miles over mountain passes through the land of the Basque people. Then the path crosses the high plains of the Navarra region and traverses the mountains of Cantabria and into the Province of Galicia. All the while, as mentioned, following very closely the same route the apostle James took on his final westward missionary journey across the Iberian Peninsula.

Pilgrims who complete the Way of St. James for religious reasons do their best to pray and attend Mass as often as possible at one of the hundreds of churches and magnificent cathedrals that line the route. You can walk as much or as little of the route as you wish. However, if you want to receive a

The Way of St. James

Compostela, you must walk the last sixty miles continuously. (A Compostela is a certificate of achievement given to pilgrims upon completion of the Way of Saint James. Besides being physical proof that a pilgrim has, indeed, completed the Way of St. James, one additional benefit of this parchment is that it will allow the bearer—providing he/she doesn't commit any mortal sins—to skip purgatory after death and proceed directly to heaven.

After receiving the Compostela, both pilgrims and

tourists alike attend the Pilgrim's Mass at the Cathedral of St. James. Other than the solemness of the Mass itself, one of the great sights is to watch the cathedral's famous swinging of a 120-pound *botafumeiro* (incense burner) spewing the pungent odor of frankincense arcing high above their heads at the Mass's completion. The final obligatory tradition is to climb up the stairway behind the main altar built over the grave of Saint James, stand behind the statue of a likeness of the good apostle, and then give him a big hug.

My Wife Hugging the Statue of St. James

Saint Matthew and the Angel
by Simone Cantarini

Chapter Nine
The Apostle Matthew

41 yrs

> As Jesus went on from there, he saw a man named Matthew
> sitting at the tax collector's booth. "Follow me," He told him,
> and Matthew got up and followed Him. Matthew 9:9 NIV

The apostle Matthew is mentioned by name in all four
lists of the Twelve Apostles in the Gospels and Acts and in
Matthew 9, where he is called by Jesus. He is also referred to as
Levi in Mark 2:14 and Luke 5:27. As we have seen, this
Matthew/Levi, two-different-name phenomenon which was not
uncommon in the New Testament Gospels, has led to some
confusion over the past two millennia. However, in the case of
Matthew/Levi, there is total agreement among scholars that the
two men are one and the same.

Matthew was born a Galilean and is described as being
the son of a man named Alphaeus. There is some confusion
among theologians and scholars as to whether or not this is the
same Alphaeus who is also mentioned as the father of the
apostle James the Less. This would make James and Matthew
either brothers or stepbrothers. The general consensus,
however, is that this is not the case, that there are two different
men named Alphaeus. The greatest evidence for this is that
whenever there is a genuine brother kinship, the Gospels clearly
state this relationship. The two best examples of this are that of
Andrew and Peter and of James the Greater and John.

At the time of his calling by Jesus, Matthew was in
Capernaum and was employed by the Roman government as a
customs duty collector—that is, a tax collector. As a Jew
extorting his fellow Jews on behalf of the governor, the future
apostle would have been reviled by both his fellow countrymen

The Calling of St. Matthew
By Caravaggio

and the Jerusalem Pharisees. This hatred for Matthew by the Jews was demonstrated during the Gospel episode in Luke 5:31–32, where Jesus told the scolding Pharisees, "It is not the healthy who need a doctor, but the sick. I have not come to call the righteous, but sinners to repentance."

After these few passages from the New Testament, Matthew's name then disappears. Like all others of the Twelve, we can be sure that from the moment of his calling until the time of the Lord's ascension that he faithfully accompanied Jesus during His entire earthly ministry. However, as a learned man, fluent in Greek, Aramaic, and Hebrew, the apostle would ultimately gain eternal renown as the author of the first of the four Gospel books, the book of Matthew. This last statement, like everything else that I discovered in the course of writing this book, is not without some controversy and confusion among modern scholars. The most radical of these theories has concluded that the apostle Matthew was not even the author of his gospel at all.

With the greatest of respect to these learned men and women, I've read their arguments about the book of Mark being the template for the books of Matthew and Luke, as well as of there being an additional, mysterious — yet undiscovered — author, "Q," and find their conclusions rather weak. For them to simply and to categorically dismiss almost 1,900 years of Church tradition is academic arrogance at the least and blatant historical revisionism at its worst. Here is why.

As early as the second century, Clement of Alexandria (150–215 AD) stated that after Pentecost, Matthew remained in Jerusalem and the local region of Judea for fifteen years. This would mean that as one of the original Twelve, he would have been a witness to the martyrdom of his fellow apostle, James the Greater, and of the ascendancy of another fellow apostle, James the Less, to the first bishop of Jerusalem.

He would be well aware of the work being done among the Gentiles by Peter and of a former enemy, Paul of Tarsus. The bishop and early Church Father, Papias of Hierapolis (100–140 AD) is on record as saying that during this turbulent period of early Christian history, the apostle most likely collected the sayings of or about Jesus and interpreted each one the best he could.

The Church historian Eusebius of Caesarea (260–339 AD) states that the Book of Matthew was written by Matthew for the first generation of Christians still living in Judea and Samaria. Although there's some controversy among modern scholars as to whether the apostle wrote the first Gospel originally in Hebrew or Aramaic, the early Church Fathers were quite clear on the matter. St. Jerome (347–420) stated that he had personally seen early copies of the Gospel written in Hebrew. Likewise, Bishop Demetrius of Alexandria (died 232) wrote that he had seen a copy of Matthew's Gospel written in Hebrew that St. Pantaenus brought back with him from his missionary work to India that had been used by the apostle Thomas.

Bishop Demetrius

● Bishop Demetrius's official title was twelfth Pope of Alexandria & Patriarch of the See of St. Mark. This meant that he was the eleventh bishop of the Church of Alexandria in a direct line of succession from the Church's founder, the evangelist St. Mark himself. Today, the Church is divided into the Greek Orthodox Church of Alexandria, the Egyptian and Ethiopian Coptic Orthodox Churches, and the Coptic Catholic Church.

● Bishop Demetrius was instrumental in establishing the way Western Christians set the date for Easter.

Matthew's Missionary Journeys

With regards to Matthew's missionary journeys after the apostle left Jerusalem once and for all, there is a tremendous amount of confusion and contradictions among historians and the early Church Fathers as to where he preached and to the question as to where he was ultimately martyred. The two biggest factors that have led to this lack of agreement are his name, *Matthew*, and the precise definition of the word *Ethiopia*.

It seems that Matthew, the author of the book of Matthew, is often confused or conflated with another member of the original Twelve Apostles named Matthias. And it's easy to see why. Both names derive from the Hebrew term *Mattityahu* (in some references, the word is spelled *Matityahu*) meaning "Gift of God." In biblical Greek his name can be found as *Matthaios* or *Matthias*; in biblical Latin, *Mattheus* or *Matthias*; in Italian, *Matteo* or *Mattia*; and in Spanish, *Mateo* or *Matías*. The second reason for the confusion has to do with the exact historical location of Ethiopia in the ancient world. This small detail is important to understand because although he is thought to have preached in many places, Matthew is considered by the vast majority of historians and theologians as the apostle of Ethiopia and Egypt.

The word *Ethiopia* is a compound Greek word. *Aitho*, means "I burn," and *ops*, means "face": "burnt face." Since the days of the Greek poet Homer, Ethiopia was the land of dark-skinned people who inhabited what is today known as the Horn of Africa. As time went on, some of the early Church Fathers mistakenly expanded the definition of Ethiopia to include all known dark-skin occupied territory south and east of the Nile River to the Red Sea, and then all the way to the subcontinent of India. But even worse—and with absolutely no historical precedent—modern-day, Internet "copy-and-paste" New Testament researchers and commentators help perpetuate the notion of an Asiatic Ethiopia that occupied the region south of the Caspian Sea, the area of ancient Persia and today's country of Iran.

But even with all of this confusion surrounding Matthew's missionary journeys, with great effort I was able to piece together what many of the ancient commentators had to say. After doing so, a fairly consistent picture emerges that supports the historical claims that designated him the apostle of Ethiopia. Equally clear is the location of his martyrdom in Alexandria, Egypt.

As just mentioned, Bishop Clement of Alexandria wrote that Matthew remained in Jerusalem and the region of Judea for fifteen years after the Resurrection of Jesus. This would have the apostle leaving town for the last time probably just after the Apostolic Council of 50 AD. If the traditional date of his martyrdom is 74 AD, this would have given him twenty-four years to complete his mission. This same Bishop Clement then stated that Matthew preached the Gospel to the Syrians, Persians, and the Ethiopians. It is very possible that during an extended stay in the ancient Syrian city of Antioch (today located in modern Turkey) he composed the Gospel that still bears his name.

But Africa would be Matthew's ultimate calling. Ambrose, bishop of Milan (340–397), and the Church historian,

Socrates of Constantinople (380-439 AD), both state explicitly that during the division of missionary territories that each of the Twelve would receive, Matthew was allotted Ethiopia.

According to a tradition within the Ethiopian Christian Church, Matthew's first journey to Ethiopia was to the city of Axum, the capital of the Aksumite Empire. Traveling centuries-old trade routes, his journey southward would have taken him down the Arabian Red Sea coast where he would have evangelized at the great Jewish communities and trading centers of Petra (in modern-day Jordan), both Medina and Mecca (modern-day Saudi Arabia), and Sana'a (the very heart of the frankincense trade located in modern-day Yemen). This journey took the apostle three years. From there it was only a short sea voyage westward across the Red Sea to Axum.

The Ark of the Covenant

- There are two cases that can be made for the actual biblical Ark of the Covenant being located in the modern-day Ethiopian city of Axum. The Ethiopian Coptic Church believes that in the time of King Solomon an Ethiopian princess named Makeda, who would later become known to history as the Queen of Sheba, visited the king and became his wife. From this union a son named Menelik was born. The queen then returned to Ethiopia, leaving their son to be raised by his father.
- Menelik I became a devoted follower of Yahweh. Upon seeing that King Solomon in his old age was falling away from the Lord and was actually desecrating the Temple in Jerusalem, he stole the Ark of the Covenant from the Holy of the Holies, sailed up the Nile River, and then the Blue Nile to Lake Tana in the Ethiopian highlands. Over the course of the next several hundred years, the Ark made its way to Axum and the Church of Our Lady Mary of Zion, where it rests today.
- The Solomonic dynasty founded by this son of the Queen of Sheba and King Solomon would rule Ethiopia for 225 generations, first as a Jewish empire and then as a Christian one. This reign would end with the death of Emperor Haile Selassie in 1974.
- A second alternative — but less romantic — for the actual biblical Ark of the Covenant being located in the city of Axum is proposed by the author Graham Hancock in his outstanding book, *The Sign and the Seal*. This author's account differs in that he has the Ark being removed from the Temple in Jerusalem by temple priests during the reign of King Manasseh of Judah around 650 BC, 200 years later than the time of King Solomon.

Arriving in 51 AD, it was in Axum that he was welcomed and greatly honored by the Ethiopian eunuch who was baptized years before by Philip the Deacon (Acts 26–40) on the road between Gaza and Jerusalem. And as an ancestral Jew, another possible draw for Matthew to choose to visit this city that is never ever mentioned was to investigate the likely true legend—a belief that still exists to this very day—that the city of Axum is the home of the original biblical Ark of the Covenant.

Apocryphal stories of Matthew's good works among the peoples of Ethiopia and the general region of the Horn of Africa may contain some grains of truth. These include encounters with malevolent and diabolical magicians and of being rescued by his fellow apostle, Andrew, from cannibals. It is said that he managed to convert the entire country to Christianity by bringing back to life the king's daughter, Iphigenia. There are also stories that he made occasional missionary trips to Egypt, possibly even to the port city of Alexandria, where he may have worked with his fellow
evangelist and the first bishop of Alexandria, St. Mark.

Coptic Church tradition says that Matthew preached in Ethiopia for twenty-three years before traveling one last time to Egypt and the city of Alexandria; the year was around 70 AD. The land route from the Ethiopian highlands was a well-established trading route that followed the Blue Nile from where the river starts at Lake Tana down to the ancient kingdom of Nubia (modern-day Sudan). Here at the present-day city of Khartoum, the Blue Nile joins with the White Nile to form the actual Nile River, which would be navigable all the way to Alexandria. One additional benefit of the journey would be to preach to the many great Jewish communities located along the river as he sailed northward: Elephantine Island, Oxyrhynchus, Crocodilopolis, Cairo, Athribis, and Schedia.

It is at Alexandria where Matthew's life story becomes a little bit more well-known. Some interpretations of the Babylonian Talmud state that the apostle was condemned to death by the Jewish Sanhedrin of Alexandria. Of all of the sensational and bizarre claims to the martyrdom of Matthew, this one makes the most sense logically, both for the cause of his death and the well-documented story of the postmortem journey of the apostle's mortal remains.

The date of his arrival in Alexandria was around 70 AD, the same year as the destruction of the second Temple in Jerusalem by the Roman armies of Emperor Vespasian and his son Titus. The most likely reason the apostle stayed on in Alexandria was to continue the work of his fellow evangelist, Mark, who was martyred in that city just a couple of years before in 68 AD. History is silent as to why Matthew was put to death in the year 74 AD. Perhaps there was still a collective memory of his early years as a despised tax collector; possibly the Jewish leaders saw his death as an appeasement to the new Roman emperor; or maybe the zeal with which this great man of God was spreading the good news of Jesus Christ was more than the leaders of the Sanhedrin could any longer tolerate.

Visiting the Earthly Remains of the Apostle Matthew Today

For the last 1,000 years, the majority of the bones of Matthew have rested in the crypt below the main altar in the Cathedral of San Matteo (St. Matthew) in Salerno, Italy. The history of how they arrived at this western Italian seaport is plagued with legend and conflicting accounts of their journey. But there are a few events and facts that share a common thread, and what follows is my attempt to produce a reliable timetable for their journey.

The story begins in the western French Atlantic coast region of Brittany. There, in the year 555, a Breton monk from the town of Gerber — who would be later known as Saint Tanguy of Locmazhé — founded a monastery on a remote spot of land that is today known as Point St. Matthew. He dedicated the abbey to Matthew the Evangelist. According to legend, since its founding, the monks of this cliff-top abbey have kept a perpetual fire burning during the night and at times of severe weather to aid the sailors of the treacherous sea off Cape Breton. A lighthouse built at the base of the ruins of St. Matthew's Abbey continues to serve mariners rounding the cape to this very day.

After his martyrdom in Alexandria, Matthew's early Christian followers spirited away the body of their beloved apostle to the then backwater city of Cairo, where a community had been established years before by Mark. There his mortal remains rested until the ninth century, protected first by the Roman Christians and then later by the Egyptian Coptic Church. Next, according to a very credible local tradition, to prevent their desecration by the Muslim conquerors—and to honor the abbey and the monks who labored to save their lives—Breton sailors voyaged to Egypt sometime around 864 to rescue the remains of their patron saint.

St. Matthew's Abby, Brittany, France
Shutterstock

It was here on the lonely Atlantic French coast of Brittany at St. Matthew's Abbey that the entirety of the apostle's bones would rest peacefully for the next 200 years. The presence of Matthew's earthly remains at the monastery would bring great fame and fortune to the abbey and its monks. Later in its history, the abbey would be taken over by the Benedictine Order and become (with a slight change) a place of sacred pilgrimage. This fame would last until the dissolution of the monasteries and destruction of the Catholic churches in 1536 by King Henry VIII.

The slight change alluded to above was brought about in the mid-eleventh century by the Norman adventurer, warlord, and, later, self-declared duke, Sir Robert Guiscard. Observing that cities of the southern tip of the Italian peninsula had been greatly weakened by unceasing internal power struggles, ineffective leadership, and harassing attacks by Saracen sailors, Guiscard besieged and captured the city of Salerno in 1076. With the blessings of Pope Nicholas II, he immediately declared himself Duke of Calabria, Apulia, and the soon-to-be kingdom of Sicily. At the same time he commissioned the building of the great cathedral that exists in Salerno to this day.

Wanting it to be as grand an edifice as possible, and knowing of the great fame that comes from possessing the holy relics of a great saint, at the same time he laid the cornerstone of his new church, Guiscard had the bones of St. Matthew brought from his native France to Salerno. The translation of the apostle's remains was not, however, a total one. As stated, the abbey had great notoriety and wealth as a result of the relics, and it is not likely they gave them up voluntarily. And so, as a concession to the monks—who probably implored Pope Nicholas to intercede on their behalf—Matthew's skull was left behind. It is documented to have still been seen at the abbey for another 400 years, after which it seems to have disappeared.

Whatever happened to this precious relic of the apostle and evangelist St. Matthew is a matter of great speculation, involving everything from being purposely thrown into the sea

Basilica of St. Matthew, Salerno, Italy

Tomb of the Apostle Matthew

by the British when they controlled Brittany during the Hundred Years War to a sudden and unfortunate cliff-side erosion wiping out the chapel in which the relic was contained.

One recent theory has the skull being spirited away — with great intrigue — from St. Matthew's Abbey in Brittany and then taken to Scotland. Here the skull was secretly kept in a crypt beneath a fifteenth-century church specially built whose former name was the Collegiate Chapel of St. Matthew. Today, this church is better known (per the author Dan Brown's novel: *The Da Vinci Code*) as the world-famous Rosslyn Chapel.

The relic, theoretically, is still there today along with — depending on which legend you want to believe — the original Scottish crown jewels, the Holy Grail, the Ark of the Covenant, or the lost treasure of the Knights Templar.

Rosslyn Chapel, Scotland
Shutterstock

The Apostle Matthias

Chapter Ten

The Apostle Matthias

30 yrs.

Then they prayed, "Lord, you know everyone's heart. Show us which of these two you have chosen to take over this apostolic ministry, which Judas left to go where he belongs." Then they cast lots, and the lot fell to Matthias; so he was added to the eleven apostles. Acts 24–26 NIV

Of all of the Twelve Apostles featured in this book, Matthias, I believe, is given the least respect. He is, of course, not listed in any of the four Gospels and doesn't even make an appearance until the Book of Acts. I even found out that there exists a minor tradition that says the apostle Peter acted too hastily in his replacement of Judas Iscariot with Matthias. Some throughout history have said that if he had waited, that Paul would have been a better candidate. Even as I write this book, it has been difficult getting a good pictorial or sculptural representation of him. Regardless, however, of what these few people may feel about the whole thing, Matthias would go on to selflessly serve his lifelong friend and Lord, Jesus, performing his duties as an apostle with great dedication and distinction and, ultimately, with his martyrdom.

Right after the ascension of Jesus and just before the first Christian Pentecost, the apostle Peter makes the case in the beginning chapter of The Acts of the Apostles for the need to elect someone to replace the now-deceased, former member of the Twelve, Judas Iscariot. He clearly stated that this person must have been with Jesus from the moment of Jesus's baptism until His ascension. Only two members of the assembled 120 followers on that springtime day in Jerusalem met these strict criteria: Matthias and Joseph, also called Barsabas. In the book, *The Golden Legend*, St. Denis (bishop of Paris, died 250 AD) said that just before the final vote was taken, a beam of brilliance shone down upon Matthias, making the choice almost a divine one.

The Western Church says very little about Matthias after his election to the Twelve in the book of Acts. Due to the criteria set by his fellow apostle Peter before his election to the Twelve, we can be sure the future apostle was with Jesus at the Jordan River on the day His Father in Heaven said, "This is my Son, whom I love; with him I am well pleased." Matthias would have been with Him as He traveled Galilee, preaching and performing miracles and sharing His insights into the kingdom of God. He, like the rest of the Twelve and the multitude of disciples, very likely abandoned the Lord as He suffered His Passion but later rejoiced at seeing Him rise to His glory into heaven.

But as little as there is in the Western Church with regards to Matthias, there is a very rich tradition with regards to the apostle in the Eastern and Orthodox Churches. He is one of five of the Twelve Apostles from whom their various churches have been given their apostolic authority. It is said that he was born in Bethlehem and was of the tribe of Judea. He was taught the law of God at the feet of Simeon the Righteous, the elder who received the infant Jesus on His presentation to the Temple (Luke 2:25–35). Tradition further says that the apostle was a follower of John the Baptist and then became an adherent of Jesus after witnessing His baptism. Because of his love of Jesus and his great zeal for the Lord's work, Orthodox tradition also lists Matthias among the Seventy Disciples sent out personally by Jesus to help spread His good news (Luke 10:1).

Matthias's Missionary Journeys

Matthias departed on his spiritual mission shortly after his election to the Twelve and the first Christian Pentecost. Tradition says that he first traveled to the region of Syrian Antioch, the modern-day Turkish city of Antakya. Here, along with his fellow apostle Peter, they evangelized and helped to found what today is called the Antioch Orthodox Church. (The patriarchs of Antioch still trace an unbroken line back to Peter.)

Tradition next has Matthias traveling northward to what is today the central Turkish region of Cappadocia. The region would not have been completely hostile to the apostle's message, as it was already acquainted — on some minimal level — with the message of Christ. We know from the book of Acts that the apostle Peter mentions travelers from Cappadocia as being members of the multitudes in attendance hearing in their own tongue the good news. Peter later addresses the "exiles of the Dispersion in Pontus, Galatia, Cappadocia, Asia, and Bithynia."

Just south of the Cappadocia region was the ancient Asia Minor provence of Cilicia. It was from one of the region's otherwise unremarkable cities that her most famous son, Paul of Tarsus, would be born. It was Paul's familiarity with this part of the world that most likely brought him there on his first and third missionary journeys. And it was there that the two men would meet and share their love of Jesus and His message; Paul, from the position of hearing from Matthias of the Lord's earthly life, and in return, our apostle gaining insight from Paul of the risen Christ. In Cappadocia, as well, both Paul and Matthias would have interacted with Peter. There is even a story of Peter's brother Andrew rescuing Matthias from a prison in the Black Sea port city of Sinope (modern-day Sinop).

After his rescue, Matthias and Andrew preached for three years together in the region. It would be from Andrew that Matthias would have heard stories of the work being done by both himself and their brother apostle, Simon, in the distant mysterious kingdom of Colchis, a land that today is primarily known as the country of Georgia. As a young man growing up, Matthias may have heard of Colchis from Greek travelers passing through Jerusalem telling people tales of the exploits of Jason and the Argonauts and their quest for the Golden Fleece.

On their long walks together as they traveled from town

to town on the good Roman roads, the two apostles probably shared memories of their early days' experiences while in the wilderness with John the Baptist. They recalled their wonder and profound awe at witnessing firsthand the miracles Jesus performed and of His sharing with them the sacred Word of God. And if the truth were to be told, they may have even shared their secret fears of their upcoming missions. Their great success in what is today the modern nation of Turkey was monumental, and Christianity would thrive in the country for more than one thousand years! But their calling to spread the teachings of Jesus could not rest. After spending time in the Black Sea port of Sinope, they all said goodbye to one another for the last time. Peter and Paul were off to Rome and their eternal glory; Andrew went to Macedonia and martyrdom in Greece; and Matthias left for Colchis to die for his Lord as well.

The Martyrdom of Matthias

Both the ancient Church Fathers and modern-day researchers state that Matthias ultimately concluded his preaching of the Gospel in the area of the world now known mostly as the Republic of Georgia. However, they referred to the region by various names: Ethiopia, Pontus, Iberia, and Colchis. Before the days of quick access to Internet search engines and Google Maps, there was a lot of confusion regarding this fact. And it is easy to see why.

At the time of Matthias's mission, the Republic of Georgia roughly consisted of two parts: the kingdom of Iberia (which was often confused with modern-day Spain) in the eastern part near the Caspian Sea and the kingdom of Colchis in the western part, bordering on the Black Sea. At the time, the kingdom of Colchis extended from parts of modern-day Russia in the north to parts of the present-day country of Turkey. There was also a region around the ancient Greek/Roman city of Phasis (modern-day Ponti), located near the center of ancient Colchis, around the mouth of the river (modern-day Rioni

River) called Pontine Ethiopia.

According to the Georgian Orthodox Church, Matthias was one of five of the Twelve Apostles to evangelize their country and from whom they trace their apostolic authority: Andrew, Simon, Matthias, Jude (Thaddaeus), and Bartholomew. He would ultimately be one of two of these apostles to be martyred in this area of the world. The other was the apostle Simon, in modern-day Abkhazia. It is possible that Matthias was selected by Peter and Andrew to supplement and then replace Simon after the apostle's martyrdom in 55 AD.

Martyrdom Site of St. Matthias, Gonia, Republic of Georgia

Matthias was martyred in the year 63. When a first attempt to execute him by stoning failed, he was then beheaded by a Roman soldier's battle-ax. The reasons for his execution are lost in the mist of antiquity; however, St. Clement of Alexandria (150–215) noted one particular trait that the apostle exhibited.

According to Clement, and in his own words, "Matthias had been remarkable for instilling in his followers the necessity of the mortification of the flesh with regard to all its sensual and irregular desires, an important lesson he had received from Christ, and which he practiced assiduously on his own flesh." Perhaps, therefore, it was his zeal for the spreading the good news of Jesus that so enraged the Roman authorities—especially members of the army, many of whom were members and worshipers of the cult of Mithras.

To visit the original burial site of the apostle Matthias, you must travel to the modern-day country of Georgia to the region just south of the Black Sea port city of Batumi. There, within the ruins of the Roman fortress of Gonio, you can find the site of his martyrdom and his now-empty original grave.

St. Matthias Abbey Church, Trier, Germany

To visit the modern-day tomb of the apostle Matthias, a pilgrim needs to travel to the western German city of Trier. Brought to the city in person over 1,700 years ago by the mother of Constantine the Great (St. Helena), the majority of Matthias's earthly remains rests today in the crypt beneath a marble effigy of the apostle just below the entrance of St. Matthias Abbey Church. The tomb has the distinction of being the only final burial site of any of the Twelve Apostles located north of the Alps.

How the relics of the last-chosen of the Twelve managed to find their way to this beautiful but formerly unknown city (at least to me) is quite a story in and of itself. Located in the Moselle wine region just east of the border with Luxembourg, Trier's recent historical distinction was to have been the home of 60,000 British prisoners of war captured at Dunkirk and France at the start of World War II. But two millennia ago, Augusta Treverorum (Trier's former Latin name) was the capital of the western Roman Empire's northern territory. In the city's 400-plus-year reign as a vital Roman military and commercial center, she would ultimately be home to eight emperors—including Constantine the Great and his common-born mother, Helena.

St. Helena, as the mother of Constantine the Great, was already a Christian at the time of her emperor/son's birth. After Constantine's Edict of Milan, in which he declared complete tolerance for Christianity throughout the whole of the Roman Empire, Helena began a long pilgrimage to the Holy Land. While there, she was instrumental in rediscovering many locations in Israel associated with the life and Passion of Jesus and commissioned the construction of several churches, many still in use. But before she became "St. Helena," she had to endure a lot of deadly and scandalous political intrigue, which is where Trier/Augusta Treverorum comes into the picture.

Empress Helena was the wife of the Roman army officer and the future emperor, Constantius Chlorus. She was born in the province of Bithynia in Asia Minor (modern-day western Turkey) of common birth, a fact her husband's rivals in Rome never let her forget. Later in their marriage, in order to further his political career, Constantius divorced Helena after the birth of Constantine and married a rival's stepdaughter named Theodora. The general then sent his son and former wife to a city called Nicomedia, a region near the modern-day city of Istanbul, Turkey. There, as a member of the inner circle at the court of Emperor Diocletian, Constantine became a great military leader and political strategist.

The future emperor Constantine went on to later join his father in the Roman Empire's campaign against the Picts in York, England, where Constantius was then a junior emperor in command of the Army of Britain, Gaul, and Spain. There, young Constantine displayed such great military skill and was so loved by his men that upon the death of his father, his legions declared him an emperor. He set up his court in Trier, which was then one of the capitals of the Western Roman Empire, and immediately set to work consolidating his power. One of the first things Constantine did was to bring his mother out of forced retirement.

Constantine the Great's rise to sole, supreme emperor of the Roman Empire was not without controversy, and the civil wars, political assassinations, and all of the other ruthless behaviors that dominate the story of powerful leaders like him fill volumes of history books. However, for our purposes, the good people of the provincial capital of Augusta Treverorum embraced and fully supported the new emperor, and—much to their credit—his mother. Eventually (with some persuasion), even the elitist courtiers in Rome came to accept Helena as an empress, and she then went on to become one of the most beloved saints in Christianity.

But it was the kindness that the people of Trier showed to her when she needed it most that she remembered when it came time to share the relics of her Holy Land pilgrimage. Thanks to her, the good people have within their midst the earthly remains of the apostle Matthias. (A few of the relics also were later given to the Abbey of Santa Giustina in Padua, Italy.) And although Helena's tomb is in a church outside of Rome, the good people of the city, in turn, have honored her memory by having her skull placed in the position of high honor in the Cathedral of Trier.

Statue of St. Matthias Over His Tomb

Sarcophagus Containing the Apostle Matthias

The Apostle Thomas Holding the Instrument of His
Martyrdom

Chapter Eleven
The Apostle Thomas

39 yRs

Thomas said to Him, "Lord, we don't know where You are going, so how can we know the way?" Jesus answered, "I am the way and the truth and the life. No one comes to the Father except through Me." John 14:5–6 NIV

With the exception of the apostle Peter — and, perhaps his brother Andrew — the life of the apostle Thomas, his missionary journeys, martyrdom, and the postmortem travels of his earthly remains has the best documentation of all the rest of the Twelve. And for many reasons. There exist at least two apocryphal and relatively complete non-canonical texts: The Acts of Thomas and The Infancy Gospel of Thomas. Both were written in the first couple of centuries after the death of Jesus Christ, and they provide an insight — although occasionally fanciful — into his life and works.

Also, there is a giant swath across the center of the subcontinent of India inhabited by Christians who trace with great clarity and zeal their apostolic authority from Thomas. Although it's a little bit controversial, there is a reasonable explanation for why this memory of the apostle has remained so uncluttered after all of these last two thousand years. It is because until the voyages of the Portuguese "discovery" of India in the seventeenth century with its subsequent introduction of Roman Catholicism, the congregations that the apostle established on the subcontinent were relatively isolated.

This autonomy meant that since Thomas's day, these Churches existed essentially unaffected by the various ecumenical councils, the seemingly endless Western and Eastern Churches' internecine warfare and schisms, or either of the two Churches' constant positioning for power and control, both spiritual and secular. Important as well is the existence of many unbroken local traditions, not only in India but across the Middle East and Mediterranean area—traditions that many scholars have chosen to dismiss.

St. Thomas holding the Lance that Killed Him

Critical as well to the apostle's legacy are the writings of many of the early Church Fathers and historians —Ephrem the Syrian (306–373), Cyril of Jerusalem (313–386), Gregory of Tours (538–594)—that directly state that Thomas was the apostle of India. Also, Church tradition and iconography often shows Thomas holding a builder's square. This is because wherever the apostle established a Christian community, he built churches; that is, actual buildings. From the island of Socotra in the Indian Ocean to the modern-day city of Chennai in eastern India, wherever these church buildings are today, either still standing or in ruins, there is a collective consciousness by the local people that they were actually built by Thomas.

There is even a song that is still sung and danced by the Thomas Christians of India called the "Songs of Thomas" or "Thomma Parvam." The song describes the apostle's early works and successes with the first generation of Hindu Brahmans and was composed by the first deacon converted to Christianity named Rambaan Thomas while Thomas was still alive. For more than a thousand years the song remained as an oral tradition. It was finally written down in 1601 by another deacon named Rambaan Thomas, a 402nd-generation descendant of the first Deacon Thomas!

Nothing is known with certainty regarding the early life and calling of Thomas to the original Twelve. Although Thomas is mentioned in the lists of the Twelve Apostles in the books of Matthew, Luke, Mark, and Acts, it is from the Gospel of John that we learn the most about him. John says that he was with the Lord and the other disciples when Jesus brought Lazarus back from the dead. He was the second to the last (before Philip) of the original Twelve while at the Last Supper to ask the living Jesus a final question: "Lord, we don't know where you are going, so how can we know the way?" Thomas is also mentioned in John's Gospel as one of the five apostles (plus two unnamed disciples) whom Jesus visits at the Sea of Galilee after His Resurrection (John 21:2–3).

However, within the context of the history of all of Christianity, Thomas is most famous for his role in the Gospels of being Doubting Thomas. When Thomas was told about Jesus's Resurrection, he infamously said, "Except I shall see in his hands the print of the nails, and put my finger into the print of the nails, and thrust my hand into his side, I will not believe." Just shortly after this, when the resurrected Jesus again appears to the entire eleven remaining of the former Twelve, the Lord directly asks Thomas to "reach hither thy finger, and behold My hands; and reach hither thy hand, and

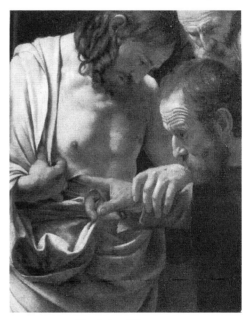

Doubting Thomas
by Caravaggio

thrust it into My side: and be not faithless, but believing."

Why Thomas was not present on that first Resurrection

appearance has been a matter of great speculation. One minor tradition says that upon witnessing the events of Jesus's crucifixion, his practical outlook on the world convinced him the Lord's mission had failed and, therefore, he simply quit. I don't agree with this explanation at all. He was (as were all of the Twelve Apostles) Jesus's friend and would simply not have abandoned Him that quickly.

Icon Depicting St. Thomas and Jesus
Icon Museum, Cyprus

The more likely reason for his absence was that, because of Thomas's sensitive nature, he was so devastated by the previous days' events that he was physically unable to join his fellows on that first Easter's evening in that Upper Room. First there was the shock of his fellow apostle Judas's betrayal. This heinous act, combined with sight of his beloved friend and precious master hanging dead and broken upon the Cross was more than he could likely bear.

In an interesting twist of fate, there was a later legend regarding Thomas in which he was the only member of the Twelve who was not present in Jerusalem at the death of the Virgin Mary. Arriving from India shortly after her burial, the apostle would find himself the only witness to her Assumption up into heaven. As she was being lifted up by the angels, she stopped long enough to undo her belt/girdle and drop it down to Thomas. He would later use the belt as a tangible proof to convince the other doubting apostles of her Assumption. It is said that Thomas kept the belt for the rest of his life, wearing it alongside his own.

Thomas's Missionary Journeys

As is the case with nearly all of the other Twelve Apostles, Thomas's precise missionary journeys are lost in the mists of time. But as I mentioned earlier, his travels have a little more historical justification than most of the others. After the first Pentecost but prior to the final dispersion of the remaining Twelve Apostles after the martyrdom of James the Greater, there is only one mention of Thomas performing any missionary work outside of the territory of Judea. This was to travel with his fellow apostle, Jude Thaddaeus, to the city of Edessa (modern Sanliurfa, Turkey) where the reigning King Abgar had invited them to preach. (Recall from the chapter on Jude/Thaddaeus that the king had originally invited Jesus.) Eusebius of Caesarea and Ephrem the Syrian support this claim. An interesting historical part of this Edessa legend is that the apostles carried with them the burial cloth from the tomb of Jesus. This burial shroud would later become known as the Shroud of Turin.

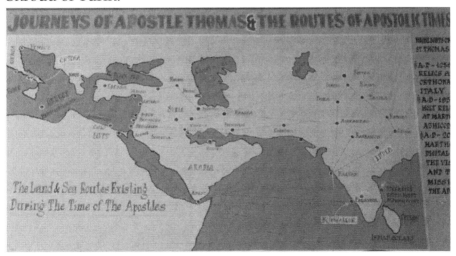

When the time came for the final departure of the Twelve after the martyrdom of James the Greater around 44 AD, Thomas's first mission would be to spread the Gospel to what was then called Parthia (roughly where Pakistan, Iran, Iraq, and Afghanistan are located). Traveling along the well-established ancient Silk Road to such ancient cities as Babylon, Baghdad, Seleucia, and Rhagae (Tehran), Thomas, along with his brother apostles Jude Thaddaeus and Bartholomew, would establish the Church of the East, also known as the Nestorian Church. Several branches of this early Church, such as the Chaldean Catholic Church and the Assyrian Church of the East trace their apostolic authority directly to the apostle Thomas.

According to the Acts of Thomas, the apostle would end this first leg of his missionary journeys in a city in northwest India (today the country of Pakistan) called Taxilla. Here he converted a local king named Gondophares to Christianity. Even though local tradition traces a continuous line of descent of apostolic authority to the apostle Thomas, this authority — as well as the Acts of Thomas itself — was completely discounted by the Western Church as a wishful fantasy. That is, until recent discoveries in archaeology have confirmed what the local congregations have known all along.

From the kingdom of Gondophares, Thomas probably traveled southward down the Indus River valley to the Indian Ocean seacoast. There he would have caught the winter trade winds, which would have carried him westward across the ocean toward the Gulf of Aden and northward into the Red Sea. He arrived back in Jerusalem in the spring of 50 AD. After attending the Apostolic Council in Jerusalem in 50 AD, Thomas left his beloved Judea for the last time and began working his way back to the subcontinent of India.

Within the tradition of the St. Thomas Christians of India, after the council, Thomas left Jerusalem with a Jewish spice merchant/guide named Abbanes and traveled the ancient Spice Route south down the Red Sea, very possibly along with his brother apostle, Matthew. The Acts of Thomas record an interesting legend regarding Thomas and Abbanes. In the story, Thomas, always the pragmatist, after having been given India as his missionary obligation, absolutely refused to accept it.

Legend says that even when Jesus appeared to him in a dream, he said no! His excuse: "By reason of the weakness of the flesh I could not travel, and I am a Hebrew man; how can I go amongst the Indians and preach the truth?" Jesus then tricked Thomas by selling him as a slave to the merchant Abbanes. The merchant then approached Thomas and asked him if Jesus was indeed his "master," and the apostle said yes. Realizing he had been tricked, he once again conceded to his Lord's will.

Upon reaching the southern Red Sea port of Aden, the two apostles parted ways with Matthew traveling westward into Ethiopia and Thomas catching the autumn Indian Ocean trade winds and sailing east. Both tradition and archaeological evidence has him stopping at Socotra, an island 300 miles south of the modern-day country of Oman, to establish a church. Thomas then continued eastward across the Indian Ocean and landed in the year 52 at the then port city of Muziris.

It was not by chance that the apostle made landfall in Muziris. He did so for at least two reasons. As it's been for centuries both before and after the time of Thomas, the port was a thriving city located on what was then known as the Spice Route. First the Arabians, then the Phoenicians, and finally Roman ships crossing the Indian Ocean from Arabia heading onward to the Spice Islands of Sumatra and Java had to stop there to provision. Likewise, the ships laden with spices and other exotic trade goods would stop there for repairs and supplies before their long westward leg back across the Indian Ocean.

There was a thriving Jewish colony there as well. Dating back to before the destruction of the First Temple in 587 BC, the Jews of Cochin (as the town is known today) were first established there as businessmen, traders, and bankers. Besides helping to support the spice trade, another very important purpose for their presence was to provide the Temple priests in Jerusalem with excellent quality cinnamon, which was then native only to the island of Sri Lanka. This cinnamon was one of five ingredients needed for the Oil of Anointing.

Thomas would remain for several years in this region, which is today the Indian state of Kerala. The Mar Thoma Church (St. Thomas) and Marthoma Pontifical Shrine located near the town of Kodungalloor both stand today at the spot where the apostle first stepped ashore on the subcontinent. The apostle would be responsible for six more churches up and down the Malabar Coast of Kerala. According to the tradition

---

Oil of Anointing

During both the First and the Second Temple periods of ancient Israel, the oil of anointing was used during the ordination of priests and the consecration of lesser temples and of the various articles of the tabernacle. Its primary purpose was to make whoever or whatever it was poured upon holy. Entire trade routes, some reaching as far as India, Indonesia, and China, were set up to supply both ancient Judaism and Christianity with the essential ingredients. One recipe for the holy oil included:

- Pure myrrh, which is the resin or sap of a tree of the *Commiphora* genus native to Oman, Yemen, Eritrea, and Ethiopia.
- Sweet cinnamon, a spice or oil extracted from from the inner bark of a tree of the genus *Cinnamomum*. It is native to the island of Sri Lanka.
- Olive oil, native to the Mediterranean Basin, is a liquid fat extracted from the fruits (olives) of the olive tree.
- Cassia is a close relative to the sweet cinnamon also known as Vietnamese or Indonesian cinnamon.
- Kaneh bosem is an unknown and rather controversial oil thought to be extracted from the cane blossom or sweet cane plant, or Indian lemon grass, all native to the Middle East. One school of thought says that the ingredient is actually an oil extracted from the cannabis plant.

---

recounted in the "Songs of Thomas," he converted the king and his extended family, many Jews, and more importantly, 3,000 Brahmin Hindus.

The St. Thomas tradition in India says that the apostle arrived in the land of the Tamil (presently the southeastern Indian state of Tamil Nadu) in 69 AD. He would have only three more years to preach the good news of Jesus before his martyrdom on a hill outside of Madras (now Chennai) in 72 AD. Within the traditions of the Indian Christians who trace their apostolic authority to Thomas, these dates are as certain as it is

Marthoma Pontifical Shrine, Kerala, India

humanly possible to know. However, when you do the math, from Thomas's arrival in Kerala in the year 52 to his arrival in the land of the Tamil would be roughly seventeen years. The region of the southern third of the tip of the Indian subcontinent that the apostle evangelized is not much larger than the U.S. state of Texas. This leads us to the question: What did Thomas do for all of those years?

The most likely answer to this question is one that until recently has been summarily dismissed by scholars as being an impossibility. This is that the apostle Thomas took literally his commission to "spread the Gospel of Jesus to the ends of the earth" and continued his missionary work all the way eastward up into China and possibly even Japan! The reasons for this shift in thinking are many.

Before I begin, I would like to remind the gentle reader of one of the guiding principles for this book that I have relied upon for a lot of my conclusions: This is the notion of local traditions. Scholars, almost by definition, have to rely on what they believe to be tangible facts. However, the trouble with "facts" is that they are often influenced and manipulated by a researcher's prejudice or the prejudices of their sources. They are influenced by their worldviews, their religious affiliations, and their occasional feelings of superiority because of their academic credentials. I need to make perfectly clear that I consider none of this a fault. As a man of science, I understand their difficulty. If they were to even remotely place their research findings in such a nebulous concept as a community's oral or written traditions, they would be laughed out of their university faculty lounges.

One of the guiding principles of the naysayers who discount Thomas's trip to China is the claim that it was physically impossible due to the amount of time needed to reach eastern China in the first century. But new research is proving that such a voyage was not only possible, it was quite common. There were oceangoing "superhighways" referred to collectively by historians as the Spice Route that were well-known to ancient mariners for hundreds of years before the birth of Christ.

A computer program that I discovered that has the ability to calculate sailing times between seaports concluded that the distance between Kerala, India (where Thomas departed), and the eastern Chinese seaport of Lianyungang (the end of the overland Silk Road) was 5,028 nautical miles. Using the most conservative figures, a sailing ship with a knowledgeable navigator who understood the currents and trade winds, and averaging two and one-half knots of speed, could complete the journey in eighty-five days. Even if it took a full year, there would be more than ample time for the apostle to make the trip.

I chose the Chinese seaport of Lianyungang in the above example because recent archaeological finds near this city have proven with reasonable certainty that the Church in China was founded by the apostle St. Thomas between 65 and 68 AD. Even if this discovery had not taken place, there has existed since the time of Thomas a — for a lack of a better term — collective consciousness in the Chaldean Church of Iraq and of the Church of the Syro-Malabar rite in southern India that he was the founder of Christianity in China. In their holy books, it is stated that "by St. Thomas, the Kingdom of Heaven took wings and flew all the way to the Chinese." Finally, and quite simply, the Chinese Orthodox Church says that they get their direct apostolic authority from the apostle Thomas.

Thomas reappears in the Indian tradition in the year 68 AD in the southeast coastal city of Madras (now modern-day

Chennai), most likely arriving at the port on a cargo-laden ship sailing westward from the Spice Islands of Indonesia. Very little is really known of his missionary work in the last years of his life. Now an old man, it is possible that he decided to withdraw

St. Thomas Mount, Chennai, India

from the world to a cave on the top of a small mountain outside the city limits in order to spend his remaining earthly days in prayer. Tradition does tell us that Thomas did greatly anger the local Hindu priests of the goddess Kali. They were either

Mural of The Martyrdom of the Apostle Thomas
St. Thome Basilica, Chennai, India

concerned about his success at converting the locals to the Good News of Jesus, or the presence of this extraordinary man of God within their midst simply offended them.

Whatever it was that Thomas did, the priests conspired to have him executed. On December 23, in the year 72 AD, while at prayer in his cave on the top of what is today referred to as St. Thomas Mount, the dedicated servant of God met his

Martyrdom Site of the Apostle Thomas.
Our Lady of Expections, Chennai, India

martyrdom by being stabbed in the back by three spears. However, these three men and their coconspirators did nothing to stem the tide of the new religion. Today, divided into at least

Detail of the Bleeding Stone of St. Thomas

seven branches, there are over seventy-one million Christians on the Indian subcontinent who directly trace their religious roots to this great man.

Today, St. Thomas Mount is located in the city of Chennai, not too far from the region's international airport. Pilgrims wanting to visit the site of Thomas's martyrdom can climb the 135 granite steps to the top of the hill or just simply drive up the long driveway. At the summit there is a large chapel built by the Portuguese in 1523 over several much older structures, dedicated to Our Lady of Expectation. Inside the church and incorporated into the altar is the stone cross carved by Thomas himself over which he fell during his martyrdom.

After his death, Thomas's followers moved his body down toward the sea and buried him under the altar of one of the churches he built. Over the centuries, dedicated parishioners and benefactors added to the original structure, and today the whole complex is incorporated into the present-day San Thome Basilica. Visitors wanting to see the original burial site of the apostle can climb down the stairs near the rear of the church and follow a long whitewashed hallway to a small chapel. There in the front of the room, closely guarded by a holy nun (whose whole purpose in life on the day I visited was to prevent anyone from taking a photograph), is an altar. Under this altar is the

San Thome Basilica, Chennai, India

former resting place of this great servant of Jesus.

I say "former resting place" because the vast majority of the bones of the holy apostle no longer reside there. But before I continue the story of the final journey of Thomas's mortal remains, I'd like to share my thoughts on this matter. Without sounding too far out of my mind, I would like to assure any pilgrim who has taken the great effort to travel to India in order to be in the presence of this great man of God, you will not be let down. He's still there! You get the absolute feeling (if you allow it in) that he's still there both in spirit and substance. It's the same with Peter at the Vatican, Bartholomew in Baskale, Philip in Hierapolis, Simon in Abkhazia, Andrew in Patras, James the Greater in Santiago, and John in Ephesus: These original burial sites still retain (for lack of a precise word) the

Original Grave of the Apostle Thomas, Chennai, India

apostles' essences, their spirits, their vitality. The molecules that made up their living bodies—flesh and blood that at one time walked with the Son of God on earth—are forever part of the makeup, strata, and chemistry of the original soil in which they were laid.

The long journey of Thomas's mortal remains to where they rest today in the Italian port city of Ortona is the most well-documented of all of the other Twelve, except for Peter. The story starts 4,500 miles away in what is today the city of Chennai, India, the site of the apostle's martyrdom. After resting in their tomb for a little less than 200 years, his remains were translated (some say they were stolen) in the year 223 AD to the ancient city of Edessa by a Christian merchant named Khabin. It is said that he left behind in India a small portion of the spear that killed the apostle and several small pieces of toe bones.

Thomas's earthly remains were ordered to be brought to Edessa by the then king, Abgar IX (some researchers' say it was Abgar X) who wished to honor the apostle of two centuries before for converting his distant relative, the original King Abgar, to Christianity. He also wished to build a memorial and great basilica worthy of veneration of the apostle's remains.

In the late forth century, the wandering monastic nun, Eugeria, wrote in her travel diary of the Basilica of St. Thomas: "We arrived at Edessa in the Name of Christ our God, and, on our arrival, we straightway repaired to the church and shrine of Saint Thomas. There, according to custom, prayers were made and the other things that were customary in the holy places were done; we read also some things concerning Saint Thomas himself. The church there is very great, very beautiful and of new construction, well worthy to be the House of God and as there was much that I desired to see, it was necessary for me to make a three days' stay there."

The church with its sacred remains would survive fires, floods, famine, earthquakes, and invasions by the Persians, the Arabs, and the Byzantines. But in 1144, a conquering Muslim army led by General Zangi captured the city. As the new governor, he turned the cathedral and shrine into first a stable and then into a mosque. Crusader armies tried unsuccessfully to recapture the city in 1144, and by 1146, the city had been completely destroyed.

Edessa's Christian community, the majority of whom were Roman Catholics, sensing the imminent destruction of their great basilica, successfully spirited the remains of the apostle out of the city. Wanting to avoid as much as possible the territories of the Byzantine Empire, they took Thomas's remains to the Mediterranean port city of Laiazzo. There, probably with the help of the navy of the Republic of Genoa, they sailed westward to the present-day Greek island of Chios. The Syrian Church celebrates the date of their arrival on the island as October 6, 1146.

The ancient city of Edessa today is the Turkish city of Sanliurfa. Located just north of the Syrian border, it is a large, prosperous city located along the upper Euphrates River, surrounded by bountiful, well-irrigated, farmland. In my research for this book, I visited there in 2011. Three sites associated with the history of Christianity were on my list: The first was to visit the traditional birthplace of the prophet Abraham and to visit the famous fish pond associated with his

The Fish Pond and Rizvaniye Mosque, Former Location of the Basilica of St. Thomas, Sanliurfa, Turkey

attempted martyrdom. The second was to explore various places associated with the first 1,200-year history of the Shroud of Turin. Finally, and most importantly, I was there to see if I could locate with absolute certainty the site of the former Basilica of St. Thomas.

Hours of research at home in books and on the Internet yielded no results. I did discover that at one time, probably as the result of the kingdom being the first in history to embrace Christianity, there were over 500 Christian churches in the city up until the Muslim conquest. Today, there are none. They were all either destroyed or converted into mosques.

The only clue I found was a short mention in Sister Eugeria's diary about the basilica being located next to the fish pond. And that turned out to still be the case almost 1,600 years later. For anyone wanting to do a pilgrimage to the former resting site of the apostle Thomas, they need to visit the region of the city where the cave of the prophet Abraham's birth and the Fish Lakes are located. There, alongside the pond, is the Rizvaniye Mosque. I knew this was the site of the original St. Thomas Basilica because there was a little bronze plaque on the entrance to the mosque that said it was so.

The Importance of Sanliurfa, Turkey

Most readers of this humble book very likely never heard of the ancient City of Edessa or, as she is known today, Sanliurfa. With regards to Christianity, this would not have been the case a little less than two thousand years ago. At that time, the city would have been on the A-list of places a pious Christian would need to make

Rizvaniye Mosque, Sanliurfa, Turkey, Site of the Former St. Thomas Basilica

• Located just north of the modern Syrian border in south/central Turkey, Edessa prospered long before the birth of Christ because of her strategic location at the crossroads of both the east/west and north/south branches of the ancient Silk Roads.

• Her greatest claim to fame is found in her modern name: Sanliurfa. The city is the biblical of Ur, the birthplace of the prophet Abraham. You can visit the cave of his birth even today.

• An additional claim to fame is the fact that she was the first city on earth to accept Christianity. As a matter of fact, her king at the time offered Jesus sanctuary from His persecutors in Jerusalem.

• In Christian times, the city had over 500 Christian churches. When my wife and I visited the city in 2011, there was not a single one left.

• Modern scholarship suggests that the Shroud of Turin spent the first 1,100 years of its existence in Edessa/Sanliurfa.

The short 100-plu-years history that Thomas's earthy remains spent on the island of Chios is lacking any verifiable details. No book or Internet source mentions any church or monastery where the relics ended up being kept. This required me to make an actual trip to this beautiful little island. While there, I learned of the Nea Moni Monastery.

Located on a mountainside seven miles inland from the island's major port city of Chios Town, the Nea Moni Monastery was built in the year 1049. According to tradition, one night three monks who were living in a cave farther up the mountain saw a bright and almost otherworldly light shining a mile below where their cave was. After a couple of days, they summoned up enough courage to hike down the mountain to where they saw the light. When they arrived at the spot, they miraculously found an icon of the Virgin Mary, hanging from the branch of a

The Nea Moni Monastery, Chios, Greece

myrtle tree. It was upon this spot that they built Nea Moni. This icon can still be seen today inside the main church. Due to the special favor of its patron, the Byzantine emperor Constantine IX, the monastery prospered greatly, becoming one of the largest in the Greek Islands. Today, the monastery is a UNESCO World Heritage site.

After exploring all of the other churches on the island, the only conclusion that can be reached is that this was the only place where the relics of the apostle Thomas could have been kept. I base this on a few different observations. The monastery was the only major religious complex on the island around the time of the sack of Edessa. The presence of the remains of Thomas would very likely add to the monastery's notoriety. Finally, in his account of the removal of the relics, Admiral Accaciuoli speaks of the church he stole them from as being on a hill just outside of the island's port city.

If, however, the exact location of the apostle's remains is not certain, their final trip to where they rest today in Ortona, Italy, is quite precise. During one of the many twelfth- and thirteenth-century wars between the various Italian republics, in order to break the stranglehold it had upon commerce in the eastern Mediterranean Sea, the Republic of Venice attacked many of the Republic of Genoa's island settlements in the region, one of which was Chios. Three galleys under the command Admiral Leone Accaciuoli from the city of Ortona attacked the island in 1258.

After sacking the island, the commander went into one of the main churches of the island to pray. While doing so, he was drawn to a divinely lit side chapel. When he asked the elderly priest who was in charge of the church about the light, he was told that the chapel held the body of the apostle Thomas. The admiral then, under the cover of darkness, assisted several of his sailors in stealing the apostle's bones, along with his headstone. As an added precaution, he took as prisoner the caretaker of the church, Father Angi Falconiero.

They all arrived with great fanfare at the port of Ortona on September 6, 1258. Here the bones have rested — rather uncomfortably — in the crypt below the altar of the Basilica-Concattedrale di San Tommaso Apostolo (Basilica of St. Thomas) for the last 750 years. They have survived an earthquake, looting of the city by the Saracen Turks in 1566, an attack by the French in 1799, and near total destruction of the basilica by the Nazis in 1943.

Basilica of St. Thomas, Ortona, Italy

Tomb of St. Thomas

Final Reflection on St. Thomas

When talking about the Twelve Apostles, if someone mentions Thomas's name, almost universally — and nearly always disparagingly — the first thought anyone has is that of the story of "Doubting Thomas." I guess if I had to admit it, this was true of me as well. But as I read and studied and researched the life of this sensitive, faithful, and loving friend of Jesus, my attitude toward him shifted. I came to the realization that this historical view of him was unfairly one-dimensional and that I needed to try to rescue him from this miscarriage of justice. I believe that a more in-depth and kinder pseudonym for Thomas should be, "The Realist!"

As I have done a few times before in my readings, I've come across writers who have written words that have expressed various aspects of the Twelve more beautifully than I ever could. The following has been borrowed, paraphrased, and annotated by me from the website: www.12.eu/thomas. I've not been able to determine the author.

For centuries St. Thomas has been represented as the patron and forerunner of all skeptics and doubters and grumblers and fault-finders. Actually, this is a gross and serious injustice to a man whose life was so bitter, and who had to suffer much distress for our sake. This skepticism and seeming lack of faith in the apostle was not so much an attitude or arrogance as it was an exemplification of that ordinary foolishness which God, in His mysterious wisdom, uses to provoke His creatures to reflect upon the majesty of divine wisdom. St. Thomas's doubt was conceived in sorrow, born in painful hesitation, and grew into a blessing. Before this apostle can be properly judged, one must remember not only that he doubted but also why his sadness made him hesitate to believe.

Thomas was the first one of the Twelve to enter the Gospels practically unnoticed, the leader of the silent, almost mute, apostles. The first seven apostles had been mentioned before their calling, but Thomas's name appears for the first time in the lists of the apostles like a ray of the sun on the edge of a forest that no one had noticed before. Although his apostolic companions stood on his right and on his left, Thomas nevertheless remained almost alone and lost in the rank and file of the apostles. Peter was the first in authority; John was the first in love. Andrew and James could sun themselves in the distinctions of their respected brothers. Philip had his happy friend Bartholomew, and Bartholomew could rely on Philip. Matthew was a rich and skilled man. James the Less, Jude Thaddeus, and Simon were closely related to the Lord, and certainly they came after Thomas. And finally, Judas Iscariot, an unpleasant and sinister character, again and again enjoyed the trust of all, in that he was permitted to carry the money purse.

One of the appearances of Thomas in the Gospels occurred immediately before the account of the raising of Lazarus from the dead. I believe that this episode from the beginning of eleventh chapter of John's Gospel reveal the true essence of Thomas's character. It was in this episode that Jesus had just fled from Jerusalem to escape stoning and seizure by the Jews. He had gone down to Perea. The grieving sisters of Lazarus, Mary and Martha of Bethany, had sent a special messenger to Him to inform Him that their brother lay very ill. To this news our Lord gave the dark and mysterious answer: "This sickness is not unto death, but for the glory of God, that through it the Son of God may be glorified." Lazarus was a very close friend of Jesus; but instead of going to him immediately, our Lord "remained two more days in the same place." Then, afterwards, he said to his disciples, "Let us go again into Judea."

The disciples were startled and confused. "Rabbi, just now the Jews were seeking to stone thee; and dost thou go there again?" And after Jesus spoke to them about the "sleep" of Lazarus, they stuck to their refusal to understand the real meaning of that word. They tried to find a plausible reason not to return where they might be noticed by the hostile Jews. "Lord, if he sleeps, he will be safe." Despite their fear and anxiety and insistence on retaining their safe position, our Lord did not hesitate to fulfill His dangerous mission of mercy. He left no doubt about the "sleep" of Lazarus. So then Jesus said to them plainly, "Lazarus is dead."

Then Thomas, the sad and faithful fellow disciple, spoke out with the bravery of a martyr. "Let us also go, that we may die with Him." Thomas, the apostle full of love and melancholy and courage! Thomas, the realist, was already expecting the worst. He was not led on by a consoling illusion, nor did he let himself be deceived, as the others, by palms or hosannas. He saw the dark storm, the darkest storm, forming on the horizon. When the Lord, despite all the urging and reminding of the disciples, wanted to "go again into Judea," Thomas was not going to let Him go alone. "Let us all go and die with Him!"

The Apostle John Holding the Cup of His Attempted
Poisoning

Chapter Twelve
The Apostle John

65 YRS

One of them, the disciple whom Jesus loved, was reclining next to him. Simon Peter motioned to this disciple and said, "Ask him which one he means." Leaning back against Jesus, he asked him, "Lord, who is it?" John 13:23–25 NIV

John, the apostle whom Jesus loved, was the youngest of all of the Twelve Apostles. He was the younger of the two sons of Zebedee and Salome and lived his early life as a fisherman in the village of Bethsaida along with his brother James the Greater. As a young adult, John (along with the apostle Andrew), was a follower of John the Baptist before the two of them became disciples of Jesus. He was the last of the Twelve to die and the only one to not have suffered a martyr's death. Recall, ironically, that his brother James would be the first of the Twelve to die.

Although historically he is always placed after his brother whenever the apostles are listed in the New Testament, John also had—along with James and the apostle Peter—what seems like an inner-circle status among all of the other followers of Jesus. The three of them were with the Lord when He raised the twelve-year-old daughter of Jairus from the dead. They stood in terror and awe at the Transfiguration when God the Father spoke from the clouds saying, "This is My Son, whom I love; with Him I am well pleased!" And although all three apostles were physically with Jesus during His Agony in Gethsemane, the Lord had to suffer alone because the three had all fallen asleep.

In the Gospels, John seems to have had another special bond with Peter as the two were often paired together on various missions. It was to John and Peter that Jesus gave the job of preparing the location for the Passover meal. It was John who most likely helped Peter gain access to the home of the high priest after the Lord's arrest. Likewise, they were the first of the remaining apostles to bear witness to Jesus's Resurrection at the empty tomb. After Christ's Ascension, the two of them (along with James the Less) took on the daunting task of the founding and nurturing of the early Church. John and Peter healed the sick and lame and served on missionary journeys together. Their zeal to spread the good news to the world even made them companions together in prison. A passage in Johann Bengel's *Commentary* sums up the relationship of these two great men perfectly: The principal apostles of the Twelve were the two, Peter and John. The former laid the foundation of the church; the latter, the crowning top stone.

And as the youngest of the Twelve, John appeared in the Gospels to also have shared an especially close and devoted relationship to Jesus. He and his brother James shared the only

Detail of the Last Supper with John Resting on Jesus's Breast

nickname given to any of the other apostles, *Boanerges*, "Sons of Thunder." John sat at the place of honor beside Jesus at the Last Supper. And most telling of all was the fact that John was the only member of the Twelve to have had the selfless dedication and unwavering courage to stay with the Lord as He died upon the Cross on that lonely hill called Calvary. And it would be to John that Jesus would give his last command as a human man: "Behold thy mother!" The apostle was also the first among the seven who were fishing in the Sea of Galilee to recognize the risen Lord having breakfast on the beach.

This special bond between Jesus and John and Peter was also highlighted by one of the more hotly debated and analyzed passages in the Gospels. In John 21, just after Jesus asks Peter three times if he loves Him, the Lord seems to suggest to the apostle the heavy price he will ultimately have to pay for his devotion. Turning toward John, Peter then asks the Lord, "Lord, what about him?" Some readers (myself included) interpret this question as simply Peter's worrying that his dear friend would be suffering the same terrifying fate and wishing out loud it was not to be. Others read it as another example of Peter's impetuousness and that he was subconsciously jealous that John might not have to suffer the same fate as himself.

Whatever the intent of Peter's question, it seemed to have strongly offended the Lord. In no uncertain terms, Jesus answered, "If I want him [John] to remain alive until I return, what is that to you? You must follow Me." This rather cryptic answer has given rise to a whole lot of different interpretations. The simplest explanation is that Jesus is telling Peter to just concentrate on his own life's destiny. That whether or not his question about John was out of true concern for his fellow apostle's welfare or out of envy or out of innocent curiosity, it was imperative that he, Peter, as Jesus's successor, must ultimately trust in His will. In other words, don't question His commands at all.

No sooner had these words left Jesus's mouth than the rumor spread among the believers that this disciple would not die (John 21:23 NIV). This New Testament passage, as expected, has given rise to volumes of interpretation and controversy. However, within the scope of this book, this passage will also have some additional importance later on in the story of John's mortal remains.

After Jesus's Resurrection, John, Peter, and a few of the other Twelve Apostles stayed in the region of Palestine, nurturing and growing the new Church. We know this from Paul, who in Galatians 2 refers to John and Peter (and James) as pillars of the Church. In the New Testament book of Acts the pair of apostles are especially singled out as healing a lame beggar at the Temple gate. This healing led to their imprisonment and subsequent trial before the rulers and elders and teachers of the law in Jerusalem. In turn, the passage opened up an opportunity for Peter to preach a sermon containing one of scriptures' famous statements that Jesus is "the stone you builders rejected which has become the cornerstone." In Acts 8, the two apostles (along with Philip the deacon) spread the Gospel to the villages of Samaria and are found confronting and subduing Simon the Magician.

The Byzantine historian Hippolytus of Thebes (later 600s AD) states that John stayed full time in the vicinity of Jerusalem and Palestine until the persecutions of the Judean King Herod Agrippa in 44 AD. Although history is silent on the matter, it is very possible he was witness as well to his brother James's death. Hippolytus also records in his *Chronicles* that John also, per Jesus's instructions from the Cross, cared for the Lord's mother, Mary, until her death and Assumption in 41 AD. He even said that the apostle purchased a house for her with an inheritance from his father Zebedee.

Shortly after the persecutions, John began the first of several missionary journeys to Asia Minor to the region of the world that is today southwestern Turkey, strengthening and helping to expand the Church of Ephesus and the surrounding cities. During this time, however, John maintained his close contact with of the mother Church in Jerusalem and continued to help provide her apostolic guidance. Although it may seem that such frequent travel would have been nearly impossible to accomplish, recent scholarship suggests this was not so. If the apostle traveled during the late spring through the early fall months, this would have been a sea voyage of about nine days' duration. If he chose instead to partake in a winter's journey overland by traveling on the existing Roman roads, the trip would have taken just over two months. Although longer, this land route would have taken the apostle through the major cities of Caesarea, Antioch, Tarsus, Iconium, and Hierapolis.

It is certain, however, that the apostle John would leave Jerusalem for the last time after the Apostolic Council around 50 AD. All traditions have him finally settling in the region of Ephesus. This date of the apostle's departure is reinforced by the fact that Paul no longer mentions meeting with the apostle in Jerusalem either after the end of his (Paul's) second missionary journey (52 AD) or the end of his third (58 AD).

The Church of Ephesus by this time was already well established in the region. Tradition says that the Church was originally founded by a group of followers of John the Baptist

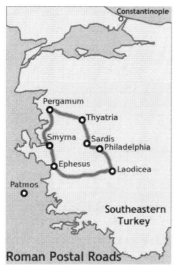

led by an unknown disciple named Apollo. The community was later reinforced by the apostle Paul. While there, John helped establish and nurture the local churches, including the ones he would later address in his book of Revelation. Using the well-established Roman postal roads, he would be able to complete a circular journey to the cities of Smyrna, Pergamum, Thyatira, Sardis, Philadelphia, and Laodicea in less than two weeks.

During this time (60–90 AD), John would write the three Epistles and the Gospel that bears his name. The success of his mission in Ephesus must have been very good because the apostle's work eventually caught the eye of the secular authorities in Rome. The emperor at the time, Domitian (81–96 AD), was a hardcore believer in the established Roman religion. He had a particular devotion to the cults of both the god Jupiter and the Roman goddess Minerva. Near the end of the emperor's reign, he instituted a series of persecutions against both Christians and Jews.

Around the year 92, John was brought to Rome, where the he was accused of the practices of prophecy, magic, and astrology. He was then condemned to death by poisoning. Many statues and paintings of John show him holding a cup in which the poison was turned into a snake, preventing him from taking a drink. In his *The Prescription of Heretics*, Tertullian of Carthage (155 AD), states that a second try at killing the apostle was attempted in which his executioners attempted to boil him in oil outside the city's Latin gate. In 493, the Basilica of San Giovanni a Porta Latina was built near the old Roman wall to commemorate the event. The nearby octagonal-shaped chapel of San Giovanni in Oleo sits on the exact location of John's attempted martyrdom.

Monastery of St. John the Theologian
Photo by Laurent Derame

Tertullian then wrote that when it was realized by the Roman authorities that trying to murder "the disciple who Jesus loved" was impossible, John was exiled to the present-day Greek island of Patmos. And it would be there in a cave on this little, otherwise uneventful spot of land off Turkey's western

Entrance to the Cave of the Apocalypse
Photo by Laurent Derame

coast that the apostle would record his divine visions for the future of mankind and his Church, which are known to the world today as the Book of Revelation. On Patmos, John would for all of humanity "bare record of the word of God, and of the testimony of Jesus Christ, and of all things that he saw" (Revelation 1:2 NIV).

According to two of his former students, Polycarp, the Bishop of Smyrna (69–156) and Ignatius of Antioch (35–108), shortly after the death of Domitian in 96 AD, John was released from his exile. He then returned home to Ephesus.

By that time, the apostle who rested his head upon the breast of his divine Master at the Last Supper was getting to be an old man. Over the course of his long life, he'd witnessed firsthand in the wilderness of Judea, the fiery preaching of John the Baptist; he

The Interior of the Cave of the Apocalypse
Photo by Laurent Derame

had stood upon the bank of the Jordan River and watched with inspired awe the mystical baptism of Jesus; he intimately shared in the glory and majesty of the Lord as He walked the earth; and as the disciple who Jesus loved, John stood steadfast in horror and despair, helplessly looking up at his friend as they hung Him upon the Cross. As a tireless servant of God, he had labored his whole life in the name of Christ's love. Having outlived twelve Roman emperors and all other members of the Twelve, John died peacefully in the year 98.

Visiting the Site of John's Tomb

Today, to visit the original tomb of the apostle John, a pilgrim needs to travel to the city of Ephesus in modern-day southwestern Turkey. No longer a port city as it was back in the apostle's time, Ephesus today is six miles inland from the sea. Visitors to the city can sail upon scheduled cruise ships into the harbor at nearby Kusadasi or fly into the Izmir Airport forty-five minutes away. Here, surrounded by the modern Turkish city of Selcuk, you find the ruins of the ancient city of Ephesus.

In the southeast corner of the old city, you will find the ruins of the huge Basilica of St. John built by the Roman Emperor Justinian and his wife Theodora. According to the Greek scholar Procopius of Caesarea (500–554 AD), the work on the gigantic building began in 548. It was built over the foundation of a much smaller church, which itself was constructed over the cave of John's death (or, as some theologians suggest, his translation). As a center of great pilgrimage when it was completed in 565, the structure rivaled in both size and beauty that of the famous Church of the Holy Apostles in Constantinople. After the Muslim invasion, the building was used as a mosque until it was completely destroyed in the fourteenth century.

The original tomb of St. John today is located where the main altar of the basilica once was located. The grave, and the cave in which he underwent his final repose, is covered by a

Ruins of the Church of St. John, Ephesus, Turkey

Original Grave of St. John, Ephesus, Turkey

large, gray marble slab topped on all four corners by Greek columns. And, as is the case of all but St. Peter, the apostle's relics are no longer there. The emperor Constantine's people were the first to discover this dilemma in the fourth century as they were trying to round up all of the relics of the Twelve Apostles for his famous Holy Apostles Church in Constantinople. This common occurrence of not finding his bones in their original burial, of course, is all well and good; however, in John's case, there is a monumental difference: As it is as well with regards to the Virgin Mary, no church, no monastery or shrine on the planet claims to possess his earthly remains!

There are two major theories as to why John's relics are missing. The first is that his bones were just simply stolen or that they were originally buried somewhere else. In 263 AD, a Germanic tribe called the Goths invaded and sacked the city of Ephesus. Having done so, they may have plundered the church built over the tomb and scattered the bones irreverently to the four winds. Or, because these central European peoples were marginally in the early stages of becoming Christians at the time of their conquest, they may have taken the bones back home with them as war booty and then have subsequently lost them.

Isa Bey Mosque, Ephesus, Turkey
by Shutterstock

As an aside, in my researches, I read that Turkish tour guides at Ephesus tell their patrons that the bones were stolen in the 1800s by British archaeologists and that they now reside in the British Museum.

The apostle scholar, Dr. William McBirnie, brought this question up with the authorities of the museum; they categorically deny the claim.

Another possibility related to this first theory is that he was originally buried someplace else. One legend states that his remains are really located in the nearby Isa Bey Mosque. Although the mosque's construction only dates back to 1375, it is possible—like many mosques throughout the Muslim world—that the building was constructed upon an older Christian foundation. I checked this possibility out firsthand during a visit to Ephesus. Because it was noontime when I arrived, both caretakers had fallen asleep in the coolness of the magnificent structure, and I had complete access to the entirety of both the building and the grounds. Nothing in my investigation showed even the slightest of a trace of any burial. I also, once they had awakened, asked both caretakers directly if they knew that John was buried there. Neither had any idea of what I was talking about.

The second big theory regarding the fate of John's mortal remains is one I have already alluded to a couple of times. That is, that John didn't actually die! The apostle/disciple "who Jesus loved" underwent some sort of translation or ascension into heaven, just like Jesus and the Virgin Mary. The foundation of this belief is that John is being kept around by God until Jesus's Second Coming, at which time the apostle will expose to the world the Antichrist. This belief is supported in some form or another by several Christian sects.

The belief of the Orthodox Church (per the apostle's expressed wishes) is that in his very old age, John wanted to be buried alive. As the story goes, John personally had his disciples dig for him a cross-shaped hole. He lay down in this hole, asked for a cloth to cover his face, and said good-bye to everyone. His disciples then covered him up with earth. The next day, when his other disciples were told of what happened, they hurriedly reopened the grave. But John was gone! Another story is told of how John, after saying good-bye to his disciples, walked into his church/cave and was swept away by a blinding light. Likewise, the Church of Latter-day Saints believes that John is, indeed, a translated being who is still working with the twelve tribes of

Israel, preparing them for the Lord's Second Coming. The Church also states that the apostle himself ordained Joseph Smith and Oliver Cowdery into their church's first priesthood (D&C 27:8), and that John was present at the endowment of the Later Day Saint's First Presidency.

Because nearly everyone to whom I mention this second theory of the possibility of John being spared the same death that all of us must someday undergo had never heard of such a thing — myself included — I felt it my responsibility to try to provide some biblical support for such a radical claim. The following attempt at an explanation is collected and summarized from many sources.

First off, the concept of *being here*, that is, being alive as a human being on this earth, and then being instantly with God without actually dying first, has some precedence in the Old Testament. And, of course, the Twelve Apostles, being educated as Jewish men, would have been aware of this. They would have known about the translation of Enoch who "walked faithfully with God; then he was no more, because God took him away" (Genesis 5:24 NIV). Also from the Old Testament, there was the story of how Elisha and the prophet Elijah "were walking along and talking together, [when] suddenly a chariot of fire and horses of fire appeared and separated the two of them, and Elijah went up to heaven in a whirlwind" (II Kings 2:11 NIV).

Likewise in the New Testament, in the Gospel of Mark (which scholars suggest is the first of the Gospels written), just after the stories of the Miracle of the Loaves and Fishes and the healing of a blind man in Bethsaida, Jesus rebukes the apostle Peter, "Get behind me, Satan! You do not have in mind the concerns of God, but merely human concerns." He continued speaking to the assembled crowds, saying, "Whoever wants to be my disciple must deny themselves and take up their cross and follow me" and then he asked the famous question: "What good is it for someone to gain the whole world, yet forfeit their soul?"

Next, Jesus said something rather cryptic. He said, "Truly I tell you, some who are standing here will not taste death before they see that the kingdom of God has come with power" (Mark 9:1 NIV). With slightly different wording, Matthew's Gospel expresses the same thing: "Truly I tell you, some who are standing here will not taste death before they see the Son of Man coming in his kingdom" (Matthew 16:28 NIV). A similar sentiment is found in Luke's Gospel as well: "Truly I tell you, some who are standing here will not taste death before they see the kingdom of God" (Luke 9:27 NIV).

The Forever Faithful Apostle John (upper left)
by Du Jardin courtesy of Shutterstock

There are, of course, a couple of points of confusion regarding the above verses. The first is that in all three Gospel passages, Jesus uses the rather unspecific word "some": "Some who are standing here will not taste death . . ." This suggests, of course, the possibility that there may be more than one person who will not die. And,

179

as it pertains to this book, the apostle John is not yet specifically singled out.

Scholarship has shed some light on the matter of the intended meaning of the words "some" and "they." But like everything else involving the apostles—and the existence of religion in general—it all boils down to how you wish to interpret their interpretations. But Jesus doesn't leave us without some explanation. For the most likely answer to this mystery, we again have our impetuous, quick-to-open-his-mouth-without-thinking, beloved apostle Peter, who helps us get some notion as to what our Lord meant.

In John's Gospel, shortly after Jesus's Resurrection, He and a group of the apostles were having breakfast next to the Sea of Galilee. When they had finished, Jesus had Peter declare three times that he loved Him and that he, Peter, would be given the task "of being a shepherd to His sheep." Then, after giving Peter some insight into the type of death he would have to undergo, Jesus said to him, "Follow Me!"

Peter, seeing that the disciple John, whom Jesus loved, was following them, asked Jesus, "Lord, and what about him?" And poor old impulsive Peter—once again—had to be admonished by his Lord. Jesus said, in no uncertain terms, "If I want him to remain until I return, what is that to you? You must follow Me!" This statement, as one can imagine, caused some discord and confusion in the minds of the apostles, so much so that John, as the author of the Gospel, felt it necessary to clarify what Jesus had said. In the end of the verse of the passage, he added: "But Jesus did not say that he would not die; He only said, 'If I want him to remain alive until I return, what is that to you?'" (John 21:13–23).

In some New Testament renderings (the King James Version, for example) the word "tarry" is used in both John 21:22 and 23 instead of the word "wait." To satisfy my own curiosity, I discovered that in the Biblical Concordances, the original Greek word for "tarry" is *parameno*. This word can be interpreted a few different ways: to remain beside; to stand; to survive; to remain alive; to endure; to abide; and to continue always near. The meanings "to remain beside" and/or "to continue always near" seem to me the most logical meaning within the context of the story.

These are the facts as I see them:

• Among the Twelve, John, his brother James, and Peter had what was an inner-circle status with Jesus.

• John seemed to have, as well, a very favored relationship with Jesus.

• We have several accounts in various Christian traditions that John did not die.

• We know that John miraculously survived at least two attempts to murder him.

• Depending on how you interpret John's Gospel, there is a strong suggestion that John would not undergo death until Jesus's Second Coming.

• When the emperor Constantine's men arrived in Ephesus to bring John's relics to Constantinople, they discovered the tomb was already empty.

• To this very day, despite my many searches to the contrary, and unlike all of the other members of the Twelve, no one church, city, or nation claims to have his relics.

And so, in summary, we are still left with only two possibilities. According to the first theory, we can only hope that some archaeological team in the future might uncover some formerly clandestine location where John's relics may actually have been buried by his followers. I don't, however, believe this will be the case because it would have been just too hard to keep such an important event a secret. Perhaps some future archaeologist, while digging in some as yet un-discovered cave along the Vistula River in Poland, will discover among the artifacts and war booty buried beside a long-gone Goth general an old earthen olive jar containing the bones of the apostle. Or maybe we can hope that someday, some obscure curator of some obscure museum in Kazakhstan or Turkmenistan will rediscover (properly labeled, of course) a pristine Middle Eastern ossuary containing the saint's bones.

Or the second of the possibilities will ultimately reveal itself. That is, that God has a special purpose for John at some near or distant future. I, personally, would like this to be the case. What thrill it would be to meet this amazing man!

The End

The production and writing of this book has been a sincere labor of love, and I'm a bit sad now that it is over. At least for now!

There is a famous quote attributed to Sir Isaac Newton, the seventeenth-century scientist, philosopher, and mathematician. "If I have seen farther than others, it is because I have stood upon the backs of giants!" And that is the case with this book. As I've mentioned before, this book is just an infinitesimally-small contribution to an already fabulously rich tradition that has over a two-thousand-year history. I hope it is found worthy.

Over the last six years of travels and researches, plus the last three years of actual writing, I've gotten to know these twelve remarkable men — men who walked upon the face of our earth with the Son of God!!! — almost as well as my own two, dear brothers. My sincerest hope is that I've lovingly and successfully shared this precious insight and knowledge with you.

Thank you

Made in the USA
San Bernardino, CA
30 May 2020

72500351R00102